ADVANCE PRAISE FOR *PEN ON FIRE*

"As women it is so often difficult for us to make space for our creative lives. We prioritize our families, our homes, the business of day-to-day existence, and expect creative work to squeeze in at the margins. Barbara DeMarco-Barrett's wonderful, practical guide teaches us to value our craft and, thus, ourselves."

—Ayelet Waldman, author of *Murder Plays House*

"We all know what it's like to have that fierce drive to do something remarkable... and no idea where or how to start. *Pen on Fire* is a beginning writer's dream cocktail of fortitude: equal parts compassion, inspiration, and fabulous limbering exercises. Want to be a writer? Drink deeply of Barbara DeMarco-Barrett's hard-earned wisdom."

—Jodi Picoult, author of *My Sister's Keeper*

"A wonderful mix of the practical and the inspirational, which can only come from a writer who knows what she's doing and what it takes to get things done."

—T. Jefferson Parker, author of *California Girl*

"A fitness gym for writers with Barbara DeMarco-Barrett, who teaches, coaxes, and cheers us on. After reading just three chapters, I somersaulted to my computer and wrote."

—Diane Leslie, author of *Fleur de Leigh's Life of Crime*

"The simple tips and easy lessons herein will provide inspiration to beginning and seasoned writers alike. I recommend it highly."

—Jo-Ann Mapson, author of *Bad Girl Creek*

pen on fire

Barbara DeMarco-Barrett

pen on fire

A Busy Woman's Guide
to Igniting the Writer Within

A Harvest Original • Harcourt, Inc.

Orlando   Austin   New York   San Diego   Toronto   London

www.HarcourtBooks.com

Library of Congress Cataloging-in-Publication Data
DeMarco-Barrett, Barbara.
Pen on fire: a busy woman's guide to igniting the writer within/Barbara
DeMarco-Barrett. — 1st ed.
p.   cm.
"A Harvest original."
ISBN 0-15-602978-2
1. Authorship — Vocational guidance.   2. Authorship.
3. Women and literature.   I. Title.
PN151.D36   2004
808'.02 — dc22   2004006316

808.02
Dema

Text set in Electra
Designed by Suzanne Fridley

Printed in the United States of America
First edition

A C E G I K J H F D B

For Brian and Travis . . . without you both,
there would be no book.

contents

tools & rituals

mining your life

craft

overcoming the obstacles

living the life

We are always afraid to start something that
we want to make very good, true, and serious.
—Brenda Ueland, IF YOU WANT TO WRITE

introduction

I t is Saturday, the fifteenth of July, early evening. Today has been nonstop. Between making phone calls, watering our parched garden, running to the library to return videos and check out more, going to the farmers market, doing laundry, and making a tray of lasagna, I doubt I remembered to breathe, much less write.

I fall into a wicker chair at the kitchen table, kick off my sandals, and take a breath, savoring a moment's respite before the next round of busyness. Any second now my son, Travis; stepson, Denney; and husband, Brian, will walk through the door, along with Brian's sister Sue and her three kids. Perhaps they'll stay for dinner, or we may all go to the fair, or at least down to the beach to watch the sunset. So why even sit down to write when I'll soon have to stop, perhaps even before I get started?

The answer swoops in: *Because I have time*, precious time, of which there is too little. I could do a million other things with these few minutes — sort through the stacks of my magazines and news-papers, which grow higher with each passing day; polish the tar-nished silver-plated pitcher that sits atop the fridge; catch up on e-mail — but I haven't yet written. So I *force* myself to sit at the kitchen table with a notebook and jot down a few words, which soon become paragraphs. By the time the crowd arrives and I have to stop, I have the beginning of something I just may want to work with.

The blank page can be the scariest aspect of writing, especially when you are beginning. All that emptiness glaring back at you — it can unnerve the hardiest of writers. Yet, in all my years of teach-ing, I've found that students overcome that fear fairly easily; as you realize you have stories inside that are yours alone, deserving to be released, you will have no problem filling pages. But the real creativity-killer — the obstacle so severe that I've seen it stop promis-ing writers before they even have a chance to begin — is time. With jobs, children, partners, and running their households to juggle, women in particular are busier than ever, with no space to nurture our creative selves.

I'm like every other woman I know: I have too much to do and too little time to do it in. I have a nine-year-old son, article deadlines, an hour-long weekly radio show interviewing writers. I edit a writers pub-lication, teach creative writing at the UC Irvine Extension, hold pri-vate writing workshops in my home, volunteer at my son's school and at church. Did I mention I also have a husband, friends, one cat, two tanks of fish, and I like to spend time reading, cooking, baking, hunt-ing for collectibles, making beaded jewelry, and walking? Finding a few hours straight, let alone an entire day, to write? Ha!

But in my experience — with my own writing as well as that of my students — the problem isn't just a lack of time. The problem is that we *tell* ourselves we need more time to write than we do. We're sure we need an hour to write anything coherent. So when we can't find that perfect hour when the phone promises to remain silent, when our loved ones are contentedly busy, and when nothing will be demanded of us, we don't write at all.

Faced by a writing project and the sprawl of free time, many of us while away the hours talking on the phone or reading magazines and newspapers, staring at the TV, going shopping or to the movies. We sit in cafés, talking, taking it all in — research, we call it. Pretty soon it's impossible to get the pen moving anymore; as time runs out and the deadline looms, paralysis sets in.

When you are starting out, or even considering becoming a writer, it's easy to feel overwhelmed. In the writing world, myths abound: Real writers, aspiring writers are told, write for an hour a day or produce a thousand words or three pages or more daily. Such prescriptions for time or page count are daunting, to say the least. Who has that much time or that much to say!

The truth is, you can get a lot done in just fifteen minutes a day. We all have at least fifteen minutes somewhere — while the pasta boils, while a child bathes, while we're on hold with the phone company or on a coffee break or at lunch. It's amazing how much you can get done when you just chip-chip-chip away at something. In fifteen minutes, you can write a page and in a year you will have the first draft of a novel. Working in fifteen-minute segments also forces you to focus, which can help you to, at the very least, get started on something.

I know this from personal experience, because my writing life changed when I started taking advantage of those extra minutes in my day. Over the years I've started (and finished) articles, stories, and poems, and even a couple of unpublished novels in those snatches of time. Recently, as I waited in the car at my son's soccer practice, I wrote a draft of a magazine column. I couldn't find writing paper anywhere in the car, but in the trunk, under the folded-up cart I use at flea markets, I found a brown shopping bag and covered its sides and bottom with a first draft.

Using fifteen-minute segments truly can start you on the road to becoming a writer. I have seen this over and over with my students: When they give even small chunks of time to writing, incredible things begin to happen. Resistance to writing evaporates and is replaced with a feeling of fun and discovery. Ideas and creativity pour out. You even begin to appreciate your writing voice and your own unique style. This was why I wrote this book: to share that transformation with even more busy women and to say, yes, it is possible to write, no matter how maxed out your life seems.

Unsure where to begin? Don't worry, I'll hold your hand every step of the way. My approach in this book is all about having fun and enjoying writing. Yes, writing is hard work, but as you work your way through these pages, you'll find that writing is *fun* hard work. There is a thrill to filling blank pages with words. When the words are flowing, few things could be better. Even professional writers I know turn to the sorts of exercises in this book because they tap into our deepest sources of creativity and make writing fun once again.

As your attitude toward time and writing changes, so will your writing habits. Seeing the pages mounting—because you've been giving your writing just a little bit of attention—you'll be inspired to write more and more often. Sometimes fifteen minutes will snowball into something grand—a half hour, an hour, or more—causing you to completely overlook the grout you meant to clean, the hydrangeas you meant to fertilize, and the pantry that desperately needs reorganizing. Tend to your writing daily, and soon finding the time to write will become second nature; when this happens you'll know you are living a writer's life.

Jodi Picoult is the author of eleven novels written in eleven years. She also has three children, a husband, and a full life. She says if she hadn't used those spare bits of time that everyone has, she never could have accomplished as much.

"Eleven years ago when I started writing professionally, I had just had a baby and was living under this gross misconception that he would sit at my feet and watch me work," says Picoult. "That was not happening! By the time I had three children, I learned I had to write in the ten minutes they were napping or when *Barney* was on TV or when they weren't hitting each other over the head with a sippy cup. At any spare moment I could, I was in front of my computer cranking something out. Because of that, I didn't have the luxury of writer's block. I actually don't buy into it. Very little of writing, in my opinion, is waiting for the muse to hit you. Quite a lot of it is sitting there and hammering it out. Some days you write beautifully and other days you just know you're cranking out garbage. But it's always easier to edit garbage than to edit a blank page. That level of discipline has stayed with me, and now, years later, when I have far more time to write, I still work on that schedule. It's being able to pick up the thread quickly and get back into where you left off."

While my son was a baby, I also learned to use minutes here and there. I longed for entire days as I once had. Yet, I found that in a few minutes I could get something done. This book, for instance, began by using nuggets of time. Certain days I was lucky to get down ten words. But using minutes when I had them kept me plugged in and kept the work fresh in my mind. It's easy to lose the momentum with your writing and so very difficult to get it back, which is why everything changes when you embrace the idea of finding fifteen minutes for your writing every day. Doing so will help you do the most important thing: Visit your work daily and keep it fresh. Janet Fitch, author of *White Oleander*, put it best when she said, "You have to keep your writing on life support, and give it oxygen."

One of the biggest challenges I've encountered since beginning teaching in 1989 is getting my students to understand that they need to spend less time *discussing* writing, worrying about not being good enough or not having the time, and more time actually putting words down on paper. There's a special relationship between a writer and her work, and as with any relationship, it takes daily tending to thrive. Even on the busiest of days, you still find time to walk your dog, cuddle your cat, play with your child, talk with your significant other, e-mail your best friend, feed your goldfish, call your mother.

So, start using those snatches of time buried in your daily routine. While the water's boiling, the coffee's dripping, during TV commercials, write. While your child bathes, sit in the bathroom with him and write about the bubbles, his babbling, his skin shiny like a seal's. As the broccoli steams, as the lasagna bakes, write about how your kitchen smells, or use that time to work on a project already under way. If you have a job outside the home, use your coffee breaks and lunchtime, or a portion of them, to write. Write while you commute. Write while waiting to see the doctor or dentist. You may not have enough time or concentration to do much of substance, but you can always make notes, record ideas, recall on paper what someone said or did that you want to remember. You have so much to say—more than you know. It's time to start getting it all down on paper.

By sharing with you how I, along with other authors, stay on the writing track, I've aimed to create a book that's both moving and practical, one that offers information and inspiration that reach far beyond my classes and radio signal, and into the hearts and minds—and fingertips—of writers everywhere. I hope that by using this book, you set your pen on fire and grow confidence in yourself as a writer. Nothing would please me more.

before
you begin

For me, writing something down was the only road out.
—Anne Tyler, in Janet Sternburg, ed.,
THE WRITER ON HER WORK

writing like there's no tomorrow

It took a while for me to get going as a writer. It wasn't until the beginning of my junior year at a private Vermont college that I knew I wanted to write, that I was desperate, actually, to be a writer. Once that knowledge took hold, there was no reconsidering my choice. I blazed along the writing path, writing hard, reading hard, making up for lost time. My advisers encouraged me. It was all good, all promising—no matter that writing was the biggest intellectual challenge of my life.

But when I graduated, the fact that I still had not transformed into Virginia Woolf or become a *New Yorker* writer sent me into a writer's block as big as Grand Central Station. It lasted a year. Finally the truth sank in: *Not* writing wasn't bringing me any closer to being like the writers I admired or to being published, and I so missed writing. I dove back in. There was no choice. I was a writer: I was miserable when I didn't write, and I wanted to write more than I wanted to do anything else. I had to write, come what may.

The deep desire to write is all you need to begin. Its power over you is bigger than the fear of rejection. Once you accept that you are a writer, you can overcome fear. I had to.

In every aspect of life, it's easy to let fear influence our decisions. We stick with jobs we hate for fear of ending up in ones that are worse. We stay in emotionally or physically abusive relationships because we are afraid to leave. And we put off writing because there's no time, we're sure we're no good, and who are we kidding, anyway? *What makes me think I'll ever make it?* This way, the dream of being a writer remains just that — a dream.

Putting aside fears in love, in life, and in writing is the only way to have a shot at achieving any measure of success.

When crime novelist Andrew Vachss came on my show, he talked about never giving up. "Spectators don't win fights, and the one fighting technique I have not seen fail yet is to just keep getting up. People shouldn't be discouraged, because they can go from everybody saying that they would never be published and all of a sudden, it's done. You never know. You're punching a wall, punching a wall, your hands are bloody and broken, and then all of a sudden the wall's down, not from any one punch but from the accumulated weight of all the punches. This is not a business for people who give up easily."

✑ set your timer

Imagine a friend has come to you for help. She dreams of becoming a writer but is burdened by fears. She worries she has no talent and has nothing to say. Perhaps she worries she's taking precious time away from her family to pursue her selfish desire to write.

For fifteen minutes, write to that friend and give her hope. Dispel each of her fears, one by one, so that when she is through talking with you and revealing her heart, she will be willing to try giving the writing life her best effort. Your words need to inspire her and help her through this difficult time.

Now, can you comfort *yourself* this way?

Imagine *you* are this person. Set the timer for fifteen minutes and, using your newfound outlook, write a letter to yourself about your plans and projects as a writer.

Be as specific as possible. What sorts of projects are you interested in? What would you like to write today? What is your ultimate goal? What is your most extravagant dream? Let what you jot down run the gamut from the most realistic project to the most outrageous imaginings. It's okay to dream on paper. In fact, writing down your goals can be a vital step toward accomplishing them.

All fruits do not ripen in one season.
—Laure Junot, duchesse d' Abrantès,
Mémoires Historiques

late bloomers

I t was my last day at my last job where I worked as a word processor at a high-tech plant that made parts for missiles. (They also
made prosthetic feet, mostly for motorcycle riders.) When I said
good-bye to Ken, a supervisor in the factory who was twenty-five
going on sixty, he said he planned to be with the company until re-
tirement. His future was spelled out for him.

"Why?" I said, befuddled. "I mean, this place makes Kevlar parts.
It's not exactly exciting stuff."

"They've got a great pension plan," he said.

"You're twenty-five!" I said.

He went on to say he felt old, that time had passed him by. And
here I was, in my midthirties and just beginning to earn a living by
writing.

When I graduated from college, I told a friend, "If I don't make
it as a writer by thirty, I'm quitting." Big surprise—I didn't make it
by thirty. I was writing fiction and poetry, and while I had been

published in small journals, I still worked as an office manager, too. It took another seven years to be writing full-time.

It troubles me when people say it's too late to pursue their dreams — whatever their dreams are. I have a cousin in Pennsylvania who loves to cook. During one of my last visits east to visit my mother in a nursing home where she spent the final year of her life, I stayed with my cousin and his family. On Sunday morning, when I returned from Mass, he had all the makings out for just about any type of breakfast. White eggs were lined up on the counter, along with a skillet, a plate of butter, bread for toasting, a box of Bisquick, potatoes, spices, nested mixing bowls, a spatula, and a carton of milk.

As I nibbled home fries, I said, "You so love to cook. Why don't you open a restaurant?" My cousin's striking blue-green eyes lit up, and then grew dim. A scowl shadowed his face.

"I'm going back to work. They called me back." He had been laid off for six months and during that time he'd begun to entertain thoughts of doing something he enjoyed. Apparently he was ready to let one phone call end that dream.

"But wouldn't you love a restaurant?" I said.

"Of course. But it's too late for that," he said. End of conversation.

Later on, his mother-in-law stopped by. The topic of my cousin's cooking came up. I repeated what I had said earlier about what a great cook he was and how he should open a restaurant.

"Oh, no!" she said. "He's going to be fifty. That's too old for a new start."

I was floored. Too late? Colonel Sanders was sixty-five when he founded KFC!

Likewise, so very many novelists published their first book in their forties and later. Diane Leslie, author of *Fleur de Leigh's Life of Crime* and *Fleur de Leigh in Exile*, says she published her first novel when she was closer to fifty than forty.

"The reasons for Fleur's late bloom (and mine)," says Leslie, "probably had to do with my having enough emotional maturity to give up caring whether or not I was competing with my writer mother. And maybe it just took forever to learn how to write. I sincerely believe that getting published later in life is best. I've appreciated it. The younger writers I know who did well took their success for granted and had a hard time when their careers began to fizzle."

Mary Rakow published her first novel, *The Memory Room*, in her early fifties. Nuala O'Faolain's bestselling first memoir, *Are You Somebody?* was published when she was in her midfifties. She had never expected it to be published much less be so well received.

"It was at that lowest point of my life," says O'Faolain, "the darkness before the dawn, that I took the opportunity to look back on my life and write about it, in a spirit of melancholy and of farewell, and then it turned out there are thousands of people out there who understood what I was writing about."

In 1962, at the age of fifty-five, Rachel Carson published *Silent Spring* and received many awards and accolades for her writing until her death two years later. Harriet Doerr launched her literary career at age seventy-three with the National Book Award–winning novel *Stones for Ibarra*, and she continued writing for almost twenty more years.

It's not all that unusual to begin writing later in life. In fact, awards and fellowships are available specifically for older women. The Ragdale Foundation, for instance, sponsors the Frances Shaw Writing Fellowship, open to women writers who begin writing seriously after age fifty-five.

Literary agent Betsy Lerner, author of *The Forest for the Trees*, says, "I just sold a first book by a woman who is sixty, and this year I sold a first book by a man in his midfifties. They'd been writing their whole lives. Sure, people love the juicy young hot thing. That said, they also really love terrific writing. No matter what age you are, if you have produced something of real beauty, of real worth, of real interest, you will get it published."

set your timer

There may be more to creative visualization, which Shakti Gawain writes about in her book by that name, than we know.

Think about what you wish for, and imagine how you'd like your life to be in six months, a year, five years from now. Your age doesn't matter here, especially if you think that you should already have realized your dream or that you're too young to see your dream come true for a good many years. Focus on the dream itself. Envision your future as you'd like to live it. Have you secretly wanted to transform a guest room or the corner of your garage into a writing studio? Write about that, down to the type of flooring it will have and the type of chair you'll sit on.

Now set your timer for fifteen minutes and write down your ideal scenario. Be specific: How will you spend your days? Do you see yourself writing full-time? What will you write — stories, articles, essays, poems, novels? Don't skimp on details. Fate may just need to know the color of the walls or the make of the car you'll drive or the design of the desk where you'll sit if it's going to fulfill your dreams.

It's important to see yourself in the sort of life you want. If you can't see yourself as a writer, how will you ever find your way there?

You cannot do good work if you take your
mind off the work to see how the community is taking it.
—Dorothy L. Sayers

hang a partition

A re writers more concerned with others' opinions of them, more given to depression, and more reluctant to share their work, especially work they consider risky, than other creative types? In my experience, yes, yes, and yes. While the painters and other visual artists I know are surely sensitive people, they also seem enviably oblivious to what others think of their work. Musicians and actors, too, have hefty egos and tend to be more obsessed with what they do than what others think *about* what they do. My husband, Brian, a professional jazz and blues guitarist, says he runs into guys all the time who can't play but want to sit in with his band. Regardless of talent, it's almost impossible to get new writers to stand up and read from their work.

Yes, writers' temperaments are unique. I have watched the most talented writers compare themselves to their favorite authors — to dead authors, especially — and grow encyclopedia-sized blocks because they believe they'll never be as good.

Talent seems to be inverse to confidence. Some of the most talented writers I know are reluctant to send out their work, so convinced are they that no one will ever publish it. Not even threats of withholding coffee or chocolate, or being condemned to write in longhand forever, can get them to print out a copy of their story, stuff it in an envelope with a self-addressed stamped envelope, and mail it off.

I encourage my students to resist negativity at all cost. In my university classes, I write on the board: NO DISCLAIMERS. I hammer it into all my students: You must shut out all the negative voices that say you'll never write as well as you hope, that you are just no good and why bother. You must hang a mental partition between you and your internal censor, the nag, the critic who says your writing stinks, and the editor who points out every little, and not-so-little, glitch. The more talented you are, the more unique your style, the harder you may have to work to block negativity and let your own voice shine through. It's no mean feat putting down words day after day, not knowing what will happen in the end.

In each class I teach, students always want to discuss publishing. They want to know how difficult it truly is to get an agent and find a publisher, and is it true that only commercial writing sells? They worry and worry that getting published is too high a bar to overcome. And these students tend to be professionals—lawyers, psychologists, teachers, programmers—people who had to work hard to get where they are and have experienced success in their fields.

I answer their questions and talk about how to get an agent and how while publishing has become harder to break into in recent years, it's always been difficult. Then I bring them back to the essence of why, hopefully, they paid to sit in my class: *Because they want to write. Because the stories they long to tell are what's important.*

Listen up: Forget about the destination—or at least lock that worry away in back of your mind. The journey is the thing. The act of writing because you love doing it, because you like how you feel when you write—that's reason enough.

And the truth is, if you keep at it long enough, if you work at your craft, take it seriously, and aim for the top, you will most likely succeed. And an element of succeeding means hanging that partition and forcing negativity to stay on the other side. Yes, I said *force*.

During the years I worked as a runner for auto parts, an Avon lady, a baker, waitress, restaurant manager, secretary, bookkeeper, and weight and stress counselor, it seemed as if I would never become a professional writer. Yet, I just had to. When you feel that strongly about something, you can't turn your back on it. You have to hang in there until it happens. And it does happen.

set your timer

Visualize a partition separating you from the glaring opinions and half-truths that stop you from writing. Set your timer for fifteen minutes and write about it. Be specific: What is the partition made of? What does it look like? Is it a curtain, a screen, or the walls of an office cubicle? Can light penetrate it? Now imagine surrounding yourself with this partition as you write. How does it feel?

That's the physical component. What about your mental partition? Write the words NO DISCLAIMERS on three-by-five cards and tape one on your computer monitor, pushpin one on your bulletin board — put them wherever you'll see them. Set your timer again for fifteen minutes and write about what you will tell yourself when the negativity tries to penetrate your creativity. It may come down to one line: *Somebody has to make it, why not me?* That's what I told my friend Billy Weiner, years ago in a car on a dark Vermont road, and I've repeated it to myself over the years when the going was rough and it looked as if I was getting nowhere with my writing.

If you don't protect yourself, you'll stop writing before you even begin. You'll look at your tablet or monitor screen and you'll say, "What's the use?" And if you don't write, you'll be miserable. You'll depress everyone around you. Your dog will stop eating. Your cat will hide under the bed. Your canaries will stop singing.

Chin up, hang that partition, and write your defense for when the voices begin.

getting started

I must govern the clock, not be governed by it.
—Golda Meir

stolen moments

When Brian and I forget to close the bedroom door at night, our cat Jo-Jo wakes me at 5:15 (I'm the one who feeds him). He does his usual number: He pads across my body as he purrs a certain predawn back-of-the-throat chortle, and I jolt awake fearing I've somehow been transported to a jungle.

I could go back to sleep if I tried, but this is the perfect time to write. The house is quiet except for the omnipresent hum of the refrigerator and the gurgling of the fish tanks. So I get up, feed Jo-Jo and the fish, make a cup of tea, and bring it to the dining-room table where I turn on the laptop or read a few pages of good writing to get my head in the right place, and I begin.

So many of us make excuses for why we can't write: no time, the kids, our job. The topic of time arises in my classes over and over. My women students, especially, grumble that there is never enough time to write and still get everything else done. Rarely do I hear a man complain about time, perhaps because—and I'm going to make a sweeping generalization here—men tend not to be the caretakers. Men make themselves and their needs a priority, after which they have time for everyone and everything else. Or if they want to write, they commit to it, and they do it—getting up early if they must, or staying up late.

But we women, we are so loaded down with commitments and obligations it's no wonder we find little time to write. Which is one reason that, when I can, I write early in the day, even before sunrise. Normal waking hours can be hellish times to get substantial creative work done, even though I try. The words come more easily before there's anything or anyone else needing my attention.

It's easy to trick yourself into thinking that once you finish whatever it is that eats up your time, you'll get to your writing. You may tell yourself that your writing will be your reward for making breakfast for everyone, cleaning the kitchen, cleaning the bathroom, running errands, doing your daily work, attending to everyone's needs, saving the planet. Instead, what will more than likely happen is you will have forgotten about your own needs—notably, the need to write.

Author Martin J. Smith says it's not about *making* time, but *taking* time. A few years ago, while he was working forty hours a week as the editor of a regional metropolitan magazine, he wrote his first two novels. He set the alarm for four A.M. and worked for two straight hours until it was time to get the kids up for school. His philosophy: If your schedule is full, then you must take time from something else, so he took it from sleep. It has worked for Smith; he's published three novels and one nonfiction book while continuing to work as a senior editor (and a very good one at that) at the *Los Angeles Times Magazine*.

Kate Braverman, author of *The Incantation of Frida K.* and *Palm Latitudes*, says, "Take your time incredibly seriously. There's this idea when you tell people you're writing, it's as if you didn't say anything to them. They keep talking, unlike if you said, 'I have to go to the office now or I'm changing a diaper or my pot is boiling over.'"

Of course, you may work best late at night after everyone has gone to bed and is fast asleep, when there is the promise of time ahead to write — for fifteen minutes or three hours. If this works for you, go for it.

That's what Susan Straight, author of the National Book Award finalist, *Highwire Moon*, does. After a day of teaching and running the master's writing program at the University of California, Riverside, when her daughters are finally in bed, she writes. "I teach all day," she says, "so I write at night. Don't say [of finding time to write] that it's a matter of structure, it's a matter of perfection, it's a matter of getting up at six. No. It's a matter of working whenever you can. I worked on my novel the other day in the van; it was a long red light. Parked cars work for me. I write around everything else."

If you cannot find stolen moments, you must face yourself and decide whether you want to write at this point in your life. On my show, short story master Ron Carlson said people who say they're addicted to writing but can't find the time to write aren't being honest. He says that it would be like an addict saying, "Oh, yeah, I'm addicted to drugs all right and I'll get around to taking drugs real soon, just as soon as I can."

Turning thirty was the tipping point for mystery writer Sara Paretsky. "It's an age where you start realizing you don't have endless time in front of you," she says. "So I thought, I'm going to write a book this year or I'm going to have to admit it's a daydream like dancing with the Bolshoi, climbing Mount Everest, or becoming fluent in French." She wrote her book — and a dozen more since.

Then there is guilt, which can be a great motivator. If you're trying to decide if you're a writer, take a look at your guilt quotient. Do you feel bad when you don't write? Do you ride yourself endlessly about how you should be writing more? And when you do write, do you feel the burden lift? Do you breathe a sigh of relief, feeling good that you got something done?

Award-winning author of the young adult novels *Downsiders, The Dark Side of Nowhere,* and *Full Tilt,* Neal Shusterman is one of the most prolific writers I know. Yet he feels guilty if he doesn't write or doesn't do something writing related during his workday.

"I have a strong work ethic," he says, "and want to feel that writing full-time is a 'real' job. I keep track of the hours I spend writing — even if they're unproductive hours. Forty hours spent working through a writer's block with no pages to show for it is still a full workweek. I don't feel guilty about that, because I know I'll also have a week where, in forty hours, I'll be on a roll and get two weeks of work done."

I can always count on novelist Jo-Ann Mapson to reduce things to their essence, including guilt. "I don't feel guilty when I don't write," she says. "I just feel as if someone cut off my hands. Incomplete. Inarticulate. And mopey."

Whether you're published or not, feeling like you haven't gotten anything done unless you've written even a paragraph is a good indication you are a writer. If you are in love with writing, or simply committed to it, you will take the time. When something is important, you find a way.

set your timer

Where do you have pockets of time? Nowhere? Then what can you give up? For two or three days, track how you spend your time. Set your timer for fifteen minutes and write about how you spend your time. Write down how much time you spend watching TV, movies, and videos or talking on the phone. How much time do you spend with friends? What about running errands, doing chores, reading magazines, cooking? Now write about how you can borrow time and use it to write. For instance, instead of running errands when they come up, perhaps you could clump them and do them on one day. And if you're the cook of the family, enlist others' help or do a lot of cooking on one day and freeze meals for later in the week.

Somewhere during your day you have at least fifteen minutes you can use to write. Start there. Try first thing in the morning, last thing at night. When are you the most lucid? The most creative? See what works. Ayelet Waldman, author of *Daughter's Keeper* and the Mommy Track mystery series, and her husband, Michael Chabon, author of *The Amazing Adventures of Kavalier and Clay*, have a brood of kids so occasionally while one writes the other sleeps or takes care of the little ones.

When writers are on deadline or immersed in a project, they become rather solitary figures out of necessity, otherwise the work would never get done. If you need to pull way back, to start taking time, do it. And don't feel guilty about it. Once you're on your way, you'll get to revert back, a little bit, anyway, to the gregarious creature you were.

*Creativity comes from trust. Trust your
instincts. And never hope more than you work.*
—Rita Mae Brown, STARTING FROM SCRATCH

freewriting shall set you free

While the blank page and the lack of time are both obstacles to writing, there's another, more insidious, threat to the beginning writer: perfectionism. For some reason new writers believe they should be better than they are, that the words should flow perfectly from the start, that they should always have lots of ideas waiting to be used.

See if this sounds familiar: You sit down to write and as the words begin to flow, you start to judge them. You cross out words or delete them. You fuss with sentences before they've even been written, and then beat yourself up for not being good enough.

In my classes I see that women have a bigger problem with this than men do, perhaps because we tend to be harder on ourselves. You need to learn to quiet that internal critic so you can be creative and allow whatever wants to come out to come out. Revision is critical—just not now. Once you have a draft, *then* it's time for revising—not before. This is where freewriting comes in.

Freewriting has been called many things: "writing practice," "stream-of-consciousness writing," "jump-starting," but these are all essentially the same thing. Freewriting is the act of writing nonstop for a preplanned period of time. You don't stop to fix grammar, misspellings, sentence structure, or to reread what you're writing. You just keep your fingers moving.

And you don't need a computer or a room with a view. All you need is paper and a writing implement. A cheap old pen and notebook will do.

The Puritans may have considered freewriting self-indulgent, but it's a constructive kind of indulgence. Rather than writing with a specific end in mind (pleasing an editor or your writing group, making money), you freewrite to loosen up, to feel good. Freewriting sparks the spontaneity and creativity that far too many people let languish from disuse. Who would want to be a Puritan when you can let your imagination soar and discover the fun, beauty, and playfulness of your own words?

When Travis was four I hosted a freewriting group. On Tuesday nights, women writers gathered around my kitchen table with notebooks and pens. To set the mood, I turned off the overhead light and switched on two rice paper lamps that sat on the counter. A candle flickered in the middle of the table and jazz played over the speakers, helping to drown out the sound of my son's videotape in the living room. We drank green tea and chitchatted for a spell; then it was time to write. We each wrote a word or phrase on a slip of paper, folded it, and dropped it into a small heart-shaped tin used only for freewriting.

Someone then picked one or two slips of paper and said the words. For the first freewrite, we set the timer for five minutes. The timer is vital as it serves as a sort of deadline that, paradoxically, allows you to forget about time.

On this particular evening, Sandy chose "lavender hour" and "not here," next to which the writer had written "all one sentence," meaning we had to write one long continuous sentence until the timer beeped, at which point we could use the imperious period.

Here's what I wrote:

At that magical hour betwixt darkness and light, the **lavender hour,** when visions of pussy willows and twigs of magenta bougainvillea dance in front of your eyes, and one thing blends into the next, this favorite time, magical purple time when, if I'm outside playing with Travis I have to stop because the ball loses its edges and Travis says, "Play ball, Mom, play," and I say, "Trav, I can't *see* the ball," but he doesn't hear this, won't pay attention to "No" and keeps saying, "Play ball, Mom," and I begin to believe that little children have better eyes, are like nocturnal creatures that see best in the dark, and the lack of light makes me feel here, but **not here,** relaxed in a way that means it's time to wind down, kick back, my butt wedged in Travis's little white resin chair on the back patio, I listen to the sounds of evening, the baby next door crying, her mother's soft reassuring voice, Brian in the kitchen, sautéing tofu, running water, other neighbors on their rooftop patio drinking wine and laughing, and then there are the smells, those same rooftop dudes with their very fashionable cigars, growing invisible mouth sores, the chocolate chip cookie smells emerging from the young mother-with-the-soft-voice's kitchen, and the smell of garlic-studded tofu and organic dandelion greens from our own golden kitchen, and Travis, picking up his baseball bat, putting the ball on the T-ball, whacking it, just missing my head, above us a rectangle of violet sky growing darker, stars showing themselves as they were light-years ago, our dog sniffing my toes, as if asking, why are you sitting in the dark, but sometimes when there is a full moon, I like to turn the lights off in the bedroom and write with the moon lighting the page and as the moon inches across the sky, I move the paper and inch across the bed, with Travis saying, "What you do, Mom?" but he understands, I know he does, because when he paints he gets this look on his face, as he fills whole pages with color, catalog pages or the comics, layering colors and says, "I make a very bootiful painting," and I remember what I read some time before I learned I was pregnant, maybe it was in an artist friend's letter to me, or in a book, that creating and sustaining a child's life is a work of art and I believe that still, that my son is a living art form, endlessly fascinating, even his little sounds when he drinks from a cup, takes a bite of a cracker, as he holds a book and tells the story as he remembers it, or bats the ball into the night sky, that each moment feeds your art and is art, if you let it be.

After the timer went off, we took turns reading. Serious comments are verboten, although spontaneous, positive reactions are fine. Three more timed writings—ten minutes, fifteen minutes, and a five-minute cooldown—and the entire freewriting practice took an hour and a half.

When you let go and practice freewriting a lot, over time you learn to stop thinking and trust the process, which is when your writing flows easily. Not all freewriting involves writing "all one sentence," but doing so encourages you to become loose and fluid. Freewriting is a superb inhibition remover. When you don't stop to think about what you're writing, your concern about whether it's good or bad vanishes, and you begin to enjoy the process of writing for what it is: the laying of words on a page.

If you're immersed in a project, you can freewrite to generate pages, as I occasionally did in writing this book. Barbara Seranella, author of the bestselling Munch Mancini mystery series, told my radio audience that the scenes in her books often begin in freewriting.

"At a recent library event," Seranella says, "I told the story of when the freewriting prompt word was 'God.' We had twenty minutes to write. After ten minutes I exhausted what I had to say about Munch and her feelings about God. Since I had ten minutes left and was supposed to keep going until the timer went off, I wrote about the detective Mace St. John's feelings about God. I ended up using that scene in my third book, *Unwanted Company*. I would never have thought of doing that otherwise. Freewriting freed me to explore other angles of my story."

If you're working on a story or an essay, try freewriting with your characters or topic in mind. It doesn't matter whether you end up using what you write or not. That's why it's best to freewrite using legal pads or inexpensive notebooks. When you want to record your thoughts or an experience, use a gorgeous journal. But when you freewrite, you need to feel free to take up lots of space — sometimes with meaningless drivel. Freewriting is about taking your writing to that loose, languid place where anything goes. It's the nudist camp for words where your writing self goes to let it all hang out.

set your timer

On slips of paper, write evocative words or phrases, fold them, and store them in a small container. I like using a miniature bonbon tin from France. It closes tightly and travels well in briefcases and totes.

Then, alone or with someone — I've done freewritings with my husband and young son — pick a time when you're relaxed and ready to have fun. Choose a word or two and set the timer for five minutes. Write whatever comes into your head. Disregard your internal editor's opinions: "Tsk, tsk, dangling participle, misspelled words, misplaced comma, tense change..."

Just write. And don't stop until the timer goes off. If you're with others, take turns reading aloud, without comment.

If you're alone, read it over silently—or aloud—then set the timer for a longer period, pick a few words, and have at it again.

Like most things in life, the main thing about starting to write is to stop dreaming and do it. Freewriting is a way to make this possible.

If you have trouble putting words on the page, use freewriting to get fired up.

When you're stuck, freewrite.

If you want writing to be fun again, freewrite. Allow your subconscious to take you on vacation—every day.

There are no new ideas. There are only new ways of making them felt.
—Audre Lorde, "Poetry Is Not a Luxury," in CHRYSALIS

load the basket, fill the jug

On a trip to India in 1986, I found myself precariously seated on the ripped brown vinyl seat of a bus shimmying up a seventeen-mile serpentine mountain road. I was on my way to Mount Abu, a tiny village midway between Delhi and Bombay, for a two-week meditation retreat.

As the bus made its ascent, we passed gaunt dark-skinned women walking barefoot along the road. They wore colorful saris and balanced bundles of wood, jugs of water, and baskets filled with rocks on the tops of their heads. The landscape was so barren and hilly; one could only imagine where they found the wood and water or why they carried rocks.

Watching these women, I thought of the writer's journey: At first it can be daunting to find the materials—the ideas—you need in what seems to be the barren landscape of your imagination and experience. But, as you look more closely, you see that it's not so barren. You find twigs and sticks and branches to keep your fire going, and you operate largely on faith that this will continue. You don't consider where you will find the wood and water tomorrow or the next day or the next week. If you did, you might lose all hope; the work would seem overwhelming. You focus on the task at hand, what needs to get done now, today. Take heart—centuries ago while men hunted, women gathered: slow work, one thing at a time. We know patience on a molecular level.

Don't trick yourself into thinking, however, that when you become a "real writer" writing will be effortless and you will no longer have to search for wood and water. When Pulitzer Prize–winning author Natalie Angier came on my radio show, I asked her if writing, at this point in her career, was easy.

"To me, writing is impossible," she said. "It just can't be done. You really have to put one foot in front of the other. I used to tell people—and I follow this advice myself—never think about the big picture. If you do, you'll be stuck with a crippling writer's block. But if you just write one word after another, pretty soon you've walked all the way across the room. That's the way I try to do it. I guess that's kind of the AA philosophy: one day at a time."

At writers' conferences and book signings, authors are almost always asked, "Where do you get your ideas?" This fascinates fledgling writers, especially those who feel they haven't done nearly enough with their lives that's the least bit exciting.

Yet, ideas abound. From where you are sitting at this very moment, you can generate more ideas than you will ever use. Scan a newspaper or magazine. Do any of the stories pique your interest? There may be another slant the writer neglected to explore or you may read a local story that is perfect for a national market. And don't forget your early life as a rich source of ideas—remember the high points and low points, the traumas and joys. (For more about this, see part 4, "Mining Your Life.")

But how do you decide which ideas are worth pursuing and which to leave behind? Of the many ideas that come, how do you know when one is sufficiently promising? Authors say the ideas they pursue are the ones they can't forget about, those that haunt them, those they think about before going to sleep, dream about, wake up pondering. Authors also write what they want to learn. Novelist Jodi Picoult says, "Sometimes the idea comes from a news story, as with *Second Glance's* eugenics movement; sometimes it comes from doing research (a conversation with a DA while researching *Salem Falls* brought me the entire plot of *Perfect Match*)." She's had ideas that came from her life as well, "like the suicidal teen I taught one year, who became the seed for *The Pact*, and arguments with my husband—such as which of us loves the other one more (*Mercy*). So, as you can see, I act like a sponge and soak up a lot of stuff because I never know which element is going to blossom into a full-fledged novel!"

Chris Bohjalian says, "If an idea isn't sufficiently jazzy to me at five in the morning when I start working, I will halt the book. I can think of three times in the last decade when I've been between sixty and two hundred pages into a novel, anywhere from three months to eight or nine months, when I said to myself, 'You know what? This idea isn't working, I've lost interest in it, I don't care passionately enough about it.' Because if I, as a novelist, don't care enough about the book to get up at 5:00 A.M. to write about it, then I'm not going to do the material sufficient justice for a reader to invest four to twenty-five hours of her life on the book."

Mystery writer Robert Ferrigno said the genesis of one of his novels, *Scavenger Hunt,* came from a blurb he read in the *Los Angeles Times* about the trend of young hip movie folk in Los Angeles who give parties and then go on scavenger hunts. The question arose in his mind: What happens when a partygoer knocks on a stranger's door, looking for an item on her list, and the door opens? From this question a crime novel blossomed.

Dreams inspire stories. Aimee Bender's short story "The Remem-berer" begins with a startling statement: "My lover is experiencing reverse evolution."

"Reverse evolution came from a dream I had many years before," says Bender. "In the dream, people became dolphins. I thought it was an interesting idea and wrote it down. Years later, its time came. That one wrote itself pretty quickly, actually."

Our pets can provide the beginnings we need, too. "Anyone who's ever lived with a dog has looked at the dog and said, 'What is going on in his head? He's watching me move through my day. What does he think of all this?'" says Carolyn Parkhurst, author of *The Dogs of Babel*. "That was part of it, certainly. I started from the characters and wanted to write about grief. It's such a universal human emo-tion; we're all scared of losing the people we love. I wanted to look at the way this character might get through that process and come out on the other side."

The first travel article I ever published was about Mount Abu, that remote Indian mountaintop village. I had traveled there three times and was obsessed with the place. It's a good thing I was obsessed, too; it took months to learn the travel-writing form, write a finished ar-ticle, write a query letter, and then face multiple rejections — as I re-call, my query received more than a dozen — before the article was finally published in *Morning Calm*.

When I was writing a biweekly magazine column, my current ob-sessions showed me what I wanted to write about. For example, I did a piece on plastic surgery when friends who had previously been against it started having all sorts of procedures done.

If you draw a blank when it comes to ideas or can't decide which ideas are worthy, it helps to brainstorm. Grab a willing friend, spouse, significant other, priest, child, or coworker, and spring for lunch. Talk about your ideas and ask for input. Or take out someone who interests you and ask to hear stories. Don't worry; it's not cheating. Writers do this all the time.

Before he begins a new novel, former Los Angeles police officer Joseph Wambaugh takes cops "who know how to talk" out to a meal. "I take four at a time to a medium-priced restaurant that serves booze," says Wambaugh, "and I buy them drinks and dinner and let them talk. I sit there and take notes. I don't use a recorder; cops are suspicious by nature. They ask me what I want to hear and I tell them, 'I don't know, but I'll know it when I hear it.'" Inevitably, an idea for a book emerges, making the cost of the dinner incidental.

Like those women with the jugs on their heads, you must attend to your work daily: It takes sheer persistence to keep your woodpile stocked up and stamina to heft the burden of fear and lethargy as you make your way along the path to becoming a writer. But attending to this act daily ensures you will always have a source of warmth.

set your timer

Do you have postcards you've collected over the years, or family photographs — either candid ones or ones so old that you're not quite sure who's in them? Flea markets and antique shops are also good sources of old postcards and family pictures for you to work with. Choose one that speaks to you, or deal them out like cards if you're working with a group. Set the timer for fifteen minutes and write, using that photo or postcard to spark your imagination. If the postcard you picked shows scenery or a street scene, what feeling or mood does it evoke? What might be happening beyond its edge, where you can't see?

If the postcard shows people, what do you imagine they are saying to one another? What is the relationship among them? Why are they dressed the way they are? Is any music playing? What just happened or is about to happen? Did they just receive good or bad news? Write from their point of view. Become them.

If you chose a candid family photo, study it carefully. What was going on in that picture? What is the subtext; what tension or meaning underlies the moment that image was recorded? Perhaps the photo is from a time in your life that continues to resonate for you, a year in which the details remain vivid and meaningful.

In the photograph, is your mother making apple strudel with her Pomeranian at her feet? What is she thinking? Is she not a cookie-making mom? Or is your father in the driveway sitting behind the wheel of his black Caddy that seemed to grow bigger as he grew older and smaller? How does he feel about that? Perhaps your brother is standing beside his first car, a turquoise Corvair convertible, and after you took the picture with your Instamatic, he put the top down and drove you to get an ice-cream cone and the ice cream got in your hair on the way home. What else do you see as you look at the photo? Does it fill you with nostalgia, remorse? What do you know now that you didn't know when the photo was taken? Write for fifteen minutes about whatever the photo inspires.

*The words! I collected them in all shapes
and sizes, and hung them like bangles in my mind.*
—Hortense Calisher, EXTREME MAGIC

harvesting words

C eladon. *Pusillanimous. Imbroglio. Ultramarine. Blackberry. Rubies. Vestige. Languishes. Crucible. Inchoate. Capitulate. Cloak.* I love words. *Most* writers love words. The feel of them on the tongue. The way they sound. Round sounds, sharp sounds, clicking sounds. There are few things more thrilling than reading a book in which the words percolate on the page. When a writer has given new life to words you've heard a million times or uses words you don't use or ordinarily think of, but love, it's inspiring.

I love reading novels that send me to the dictionary to look up words. Jonathan Franzen's *The Corrections* did this.

So did Don DeLillo's *Underworld.* I pulled out the Webster's to look up *crepuscular:* "Of, relating to, or resembling twilight: DIM . . . active during twilight <~insects>." I can never look at fireflies, now, without thinking of them as crepuscular.

Ann Patchett's *Bel Canto* yielded the word *sangfroid:* "self-possession or imperturbability esp. under strain." So, I have sangfroid when I don't stress out if I'm late getting somewhere.

Every so often I go on word jags. For instance, a few months back I felt verb-challenged, and I heard that reading the sports section was a great way to liven up your use of verbs, so every day for a week I spent time with the sports page. Perhaps more than any other type of writer, sportswriters are aware of the need for powerful, specific verbs. You'll never read on the sports page: "He was throwing the ball." Rather, "He hurled the ball through the air." I made a list—*bobbled, lingered, ladled*—as a reminder to use action verbs, the more specific the better.

I love hearing how words affect other writers. Fiction writer Ron Carlson, who publishes his short stories in *Harper's,* the *New Yorker, McCall's,* and *Esquire,* says he collects words and allows them to get into and color his work. "Most recently I used *behoove, dint,* and *deem* (each many times) in a comic commencement address," he says. "In writing fiction I will say honestly that I pay attention to every single word. A writer would. In my current notebook, I see this list: *nostrum, astringent, torpor, cosseted, riant.*"

Judith Schwartz, author of *The Mother Puzzle,* who is writing a literary historical novel, says, "I'm collecting words and phrases from the period to create a kind of 'verbal palette' to work from. In writing about turn-of-the-century Vienna, I realized that I needed a vocabulary to create the right tone, so I steeped myself in literature of the time to absorb the appropriate language. When I came across words that sounded right, I jotted them down for inspiration. Actually, the process of tuning into the language was a useful exercise in itself. And knowing it's there gives me a sense of security about it. I suppose if I get stuck I can look at it."

It's easy to notice when writers are into words. Their writing shows it. Friend and journalist CJ Bahnsen says when he reads, he makes notes of the words he likes in a little notebook or in the margin of the book or article. Later he transfers the words to a master vocabulary list on his computer. Some he ends up using in his own work; others he likes but would never use.

"Yesterday I came across *filch*, and another from a film review: *perf*. And *po-mo*...I don't know what it means. I like writing down slang as much as the real word. I get them from overheard dialogue. A guy called the street that Alta Coffee is on [in Newport Beach, California] 'revenue alley' because of all the high-end businesses there."

Collecting words, and reading for words, also helps to increase your vocabulary. When students worry about not knowing enough words, I say one word: "Read."

set your timer

Keep a notebook — or a section in your notebook — for words you come across that you love the sound of; words you'd like to use; words that simply impress you, even if you have no inclination to ever use them; and words you come across that you don't know. For a week, write down five words a day that you either read or hear spoken.

Read the works of authors who have splendid vocabularies — Cynthia Ozick, Jonathan Franzen, Michael Chabon, Don DeLillo, Kate Braverman — and write down words you either look up or simply love.

Experiment with using these words as freewriting prompts. Choose one or more of them to write about for fifteen minutes, or incorporate them into your writing and notice how they alter the tone or voice of your work.

As you write more and continue to be attuned to words, you'll find the words you use enriching your writing and giving you far more flexibility.

As Mark Twain once said, "The difference between the almost right word and the right word is really a large matter — 'tis the difference between the lightning bug and the lightning."

first lines

I deas for short stories, novels, articles, essays, books, screenplays, poems, ad infinitum, come from a multitude of places: a dream, a phrase, a feeling, an image, a first line.

First lines are fickle; they come at the most inopportune times. You may be driving down the street, bathing your dog, sweeping the floor, going for a walk, preparing a meal, or making love when a line will come to you that is stunning for its imagery or emotion. If you can possibly break away from what you're doing and scribble it somewhere, do it.

This is one reason I keep paper and pens just about *everywhere*—in my purse, the car, and all the rooms of the house. Consider keeping a notebook or a section in your organizer for this. Write down first lines as you think of them, even if you have no immediate use for them. Write them on whatever is available—cocktail napkins, candy wrappers, Post-it notes—and stash them in an expandable file or copy them into your notebook. Be sure to store your collection of first lines in a handy place so that whenever you need one you don't waste time looking. Just grab the file folder or open your notebook and there it will be, waiting to be used.

First lines are different from ideas in other forms. Good first lines hook the reader. They also hook the writer.

Aimee Bender, author of *The Girl in the Flammable Skirt*, says that her short stories typically begin with first lines. "There are a million first lines that don't work; they're just bad first lines. But if there's a first line that makes me want to know what the next line is, I'll go on that road and see what I discover from there. Sometimes you can feel in the first line a certain kind of voice of a character, so a character will come from that sentence, too."

I went to one of my bookshelves and pulled a few books with compelling first lines:

She hurries from the house, wearing a coat too heavy for the weather.

— Michael Cunningham, *The Hours*

When the lights went off the accompanist kissed her.

— Ann Patchett, *Bel Canto*

Here is what we know, those of us who can speak to tell a story: On the afternoon of October 24, my wife, Lexy Ransome, climbed to the top of the apple tree in our backyard and fell to her death.

— Carolyn Parkhurst, *The Dogs of Babel*

These first lines are powerful; they must have compelled the author to keep writing as much or more than they have driven readers to turn the page.

But what if first lines do not come? What if you draw a blank? Go to your bookshelf and randomly pick a book. Open it, shut your eyes, and let your fingertip fall on the page. Open your eyes, and wherever you're pointing, write that line down and use it as a first line.

Open the newspaper at random, point to a section of the page, and write down the first line that you see. Use ad slogans; there's sadly never any shortage. Turn on *Oprah* or any TV show — not that I am suggesting that you watch TV! — and after the commercial break, write down the first line you hear. Ask your partner or child for a first line and commit to using whatever comes out of their mouths.

And if, when you sit down to write, you draw a blank, get out the timer and freewrite to the first line. You'll know you've found it when you feel chills or have an aha! moment.

Ron Carlson uses first lines to get started and has at least one short story in his collection, *A Kind of Flying*, that developed from a first line. "In 'The Prisoner of Bluestone,'" he recalls, "I started with the sentence, 'There was a camera.' I gave it to my graduate class and we all wrote stories."

Here's how Carlson's story begins:

There was a camera. Mr. Ruckelbar was helping load the crushed sedan onto DiPaulo's tow truck when an old Nikon camera fell from the gashed trunkwell and hit him on the shoulder. At first he thought it was a rock or a taillight assembly; things had fallen on him before as he and DiPaulo had wrestled the ruined vehicles onto the tilt bed of DiPaulo's big custom Ford, and of course DiPaulo wasn't there to be hit. He had a bad back and was in the cab working the hydraulics and calling, "Good? Are we good yet?"

Carlson says that in his story, he "had the notion that the film would be developed and a secret revealed, but by the time the camera appeared, in the wreckage of a 'death car,' the story had an inventory and trajectory of its own."

Dani Shapiro, author of *Family History*, uses first lines to get her going. "First lines do lead me in," she says. "Especially with essays, I find that I need at least what I think is going to be the first sentence before I begin. When the first sentence comes to me is when I can begin. But it's important to not stay married to it."

Yes, it's fine if you end up shedding the sentence that got you started. It will have served its purpose.

Of course beginnings are more complicated than first lines. But you have to start somewhere.

set your timer

In your notebook, start a list of first lines or phrases. Lines like "I remember..." and "The saddest thing I know..." and "Try to talk your way out of this one..." are all good prompts.

Collect ad slogans and lines you've heard that resonate — for whatever reason. These might be the strangest bits of conversation you have ever heard or the most revelatory or anything in between.

Borrow first lines from articles in newspapers or magazines. Ask your child for a first line, ask the mail carrier. Say, "I need a first line for what I'm writing. Anything will do." Anything really will do; first lines don't have to be perfect sentences. Even phrases work.

When you're in need of inspiration, open your notebook or reach into your file, choose a first line, set the timer, and let it rip. If you don't know what to write, freewrite. It may lead you to a place where you've never been.

I remember what was missing instead
of what was there. I am a chronicler of absence.
—Carrie Fisher

create a written snapshot

C ameras spit out images that help us remember where we were, who we were with, moments of our lives. And while I love photographs and spent years as a photographer, writing can be an even more effective way to secure certain kinds of memories.

I have cartons full of photos taken since my son, Travis, was born nine years ago. Back then, when I held my son, I would try to memorize the line of his arm, the curve of his cheek—committing to memory tactile details. The act of writing these down helped me remember.

"I only write to remember," says Beth Kephart, author of the National Book Award nominee *A Slant of Sun*. "It is in the process of looking for a word that I find a memory—the color of a rose, the jewelry on a hand, a feeling of desolation. Writing connects us back to ourselves, loops us into what we would have forgotten had we not stopped and sat and stared out the window and looked for the only possible word that can yield again what has been lost."

Images don't always exist for the moments you want to remember, and if you don't write those moments down, they will disappear. When Travis was four, I wrote: "Travis tells me he wants to marry me someday and then 'we'll have to wear those married-type clothes.'"

How could you ever photograph your child saying that? Only words can do it.

Years from now, there's no way I will remember all the details of today. So I pay attention to what I see and hear, I write about it, and my words satisfy my writerly need to remember.

Even though National Book Award–winning poet Gerald Stern says he remembers everything, he still pays constant attention to what he sees, hears, and smells.

"It's exhausting!" he said on my show one night. "Unless I'm troubled by a problem, I sleep right through the night. Paying attention is the work. I love that. I pay attention to everything. I have an exhaustive memory; I never forget anything, why and where it happened…And I love the dawn. Now, in June, in early summer, birds go wild. The place is lush, watery, humid, hot, filled with life. I make some coffee and weep from how beautiful it is."

Stern's writing is a testament to observation. Allow yours to be, too.

When you are a writer, you are always a writer. Writing is not like a job that you report to at 8:00 and leave at 5:00 and forget about until the next day. You will find your writer's mind rarely—if ever—turns off. You may even find yourself wanting to stop in the middle of doing something to write about *what* you're doing—whether you're in the middle of dinner, a bath, or a party.

Women are used to switching tasks a million times a day, so for us natural multitaskers, writing in the midst of an experience shouldn't be a stretch and can be a fun, uninhibited way to get words down. Writing fast, writing in the midst of things, using whatever blips of time you have gives immediacy to your work and helps to break down barriers to writing.

It may seem crazy to others, your need to write in the midst of things. Friends and family who lead normal lives may not understand that someday those words you put down will help you to remember the details of a particular time in case later you want to turn it into something more.

But what you experience is important. The stories you write down, however fleetingly, are the beads that mark the time and one day may be strung together into a thing of beauty. A woman who writes learns to accept these gems.

set your timer

For fifteen minutes, stop and listen—truly listen—until even the silence is deafening. Look around you and notice everything: the objects that inhabit your home, the postcards, reminders, and magnets that stick to your fridge. Write about your kitchen walls, the bathroom rug, the wineglass with a drop of red wine left in the bottom that sits on the coffee table.

Who do you love and what do you want to remember about them? Put down details, things you might easily forget as the years pass. The way they smile shyly, as if afraid of showing all their teeth. The way they smell. The little kindnesses they do. By committing these details to paper, you commit them to memory for all time.

While in the midst of daily life—or at a party, concert, or dinner—take a personal time-out. Reach for pen and paper (or a computer), and write about what's happening in the moment. Write down what those around you are saying, even if they are talking to you. Don't worry about what they think. Don't worry, either, about punctuation, spelling, or making this writing into a story. Don't worry about it being anything other than what it is. For now, it is enough to collect the words and images.

Create a written snapshot of the moment in which you are living. Not only will you see and experience it in new ways, you'll also retain the details to savor forever. You may also find yourself in the midst of a story.

A child's attitude toward everything is an artist's attitude.
—Willa Cather

through a child's eyes and ears

On the bottom of a small white basket that holds stamps and return-address labels is a Popsicle stick with glued-on glitter that my son, Travis, made when he was four. His drawings from back then show people with wacky toothy smiles. Yesterday, we were in the car. I had just turned on the radio and it was all static. My now-nine-year-old said, "Is that a drumroll on the radio?"

Author Judith Schwartz says that when her son didn't yet know the word *sarcastic,* he would ask, "Are you being diagonal about that?"

The original way in which children see things makes me remember to be fresh in my approach, to try to say it the way I see it, not the way I think I should see it or how someone else sees it.

It's easy not to be yourself in writing. In school we learn to write in a style we otherwise never use. Our book reports are stilted, our essays stiff. They're not written in our voice—we don't even know what our voice is. But our teachers give us As for turning in work that's coherent, academic, and formal, so we get used to not sounding like ourselves. We stop seeing things with fresh eyes, with a *child's* eyes, because we worry we'll sound corny or sentimental or just plain wrong, and since we learn to care too much about what everyone thinks, we stop being original.

The company of children, or an adult who has an original way of seeing things, or a writer who strikes us with the freshness of his or her voice, reminds us to look at the world without preconception, cliché, or fear. Their originality infects us and we begin to start seeing things in a new way.

Aimee Bender began her love affair with fairy tales when she was a child. She loves them still. In graduate school, though, she tried weaning herself away from the form. "I had made up a rule that didn't exist," she says. "I felt like serious fiction had to be based in realism. It was such a loss. When I started to get back into fairy tales, it felt like such a relief. I like fairy tales so much; they live in our minds so completely in terms of storytelling and imagery. As a kid, I loved making up stories. It was a free and joyful time for writing."

You don't need to have children of your own to learn how they see. Go with a friend to pick up her kid at school. Go to birthday parties. Babysit. I love eavesdropping on children to hear their original way of speaking and how they see things. Listen. Pay attention. See as a child sees and infuse your work with that originality.

set your timer

Sit at your computer or with a pad and pen, and describe an activity (a sport, making cookies, polishing shoes), a place (the kitchen, your parents' bedroom, the school cafeteria), an item (a box of tissues, a purple ceramic pitcher, a bottle of perfume), or a living creature (a cat, a friend, the mail carrier), as though seeing it for the first time through a child's eyes.

For fifteen minutes, let your writing evoke that child. Use words a child would use. Use simple sentence structures. Make up metaphors and similes drawing on the images and language of childhood. How would a child see her own life and the lives of those around her?

Perhaps you have mementos from your childhood—a jewelry box, dolls, stuffed animals, books. Become the child who you were. Write about where these beloved objects came from and what they mean to you. Stay in the child's point of view.

Think back to what you read as a kid. Rewrite a favorite story or fairy tale, use a child's phrase as the basis for freewriting, or talk to a child about what you're working on and ask her opinion about where the story should go or what should happen next. Then, for fifteen minutes, write nonstop, using her suggestion.

making lists

One of the first things I have each of my students do is compile lists in an idea book, in a journal, or in a section of an organizer.

Lists can be a starting point when you don't know what to write about. Lists are a way to root you in the work at hand. And the lists you make become a part of your history; looking at them later will show you who you were and where you came from.

Recently I came across a list called "Favorite Foods" that I wrote down for my son just after he turned five: broccoli, tofu, greens, cantaloupe, milk. It reminded me that Travis had been in a worried-about-death phase. Nightly he cried because he was distressed by the idea that his dad and I might die before him and how would he ever take care of himself? He still could not read or write very well and he worried that if we died, he would not know how to shop and pick out his favorite foods. So he asked me to create a list he could take to the market, just in case.

Lists help to ground us in detail, help us remember—just as our lists of what we need to get done or to shop for do. And lists are a wonderful way to jump-start your creativity. You might use headers such as "People Who Look Like Their Pets," "Ridiculous Things That Go On in My Neighborhood," "Topics That Intrigue Me," and "What I Will Eat/Drink/Do When I'm Eighty." You can also list adjectives describing a character you are creating or nouns telling what your character owns, wears, and eats to help you develop that character. Lists take on lives of their own and help you excavate more than you thought possible.

Writers sometimes use lists to form a narrative, as in *The Things They Carried* by Tim O'Brien and Helen Fielding's *Bridget Jones's Diary*, and to help them organize their material. Jodi Picoult, author of *My Sister's Keeper*, says, "When I write, I never feel particularly creative. Instead, I see a succession of scenes in my head that, apparently, it's my job to translate into words so that everyone else can see them, too. To this end, when I write a chapter, I start by listing all those scenes that I know are going to be playing through my mind—and then I just write them one by one, until I get to the end of my list...which is how I know I've finished that particular chapter. I think that knowing what's coming is what helps me facilitate a smoother plot and makes me want to get to whatever's coming next on the list, in the same way (I hope!) that a reader will want to turn the pages when I'm through."

There are endless ways to use lists. See what you can come up with on your own.

set your timer

Set the timer for fifteen minutes and begin to create lists. Start with headers on separate sheets of paper. Then, beneath each one, begin to generate items.

For instance, under a list I started called "Topics for My Column," I included: "stories hairdressers hear," "women called to disaster work," "women inventors," and "ways that advertising lures women to buy."

Under "Things That Go On in My Neighborhood," I listed: "72-year-old Harmon wants to save $200 so he decides to fix his own roof, slips off, and ends up in a convalescent home for three months," and "my next-door neighbor knows we have peepers but she never pulls down the shades."

Make a list of things you dwell on, read about, or write about, such as death, sibling relationships, fidelity, or your mother. List-making is a perfect activity for those tiny moments of time — while standing in a line, at your child's swim practice, *whatever*. It requires a different sort of concentration than even a sustained freewrite and it gets you thinking creatively.

You might also consider using found lists. A friend of mine, Jennifer, collects shopping lists she finds in carts at the supermarket. I've picked up children's notes and poems that litter the playground of my son's school. I keep them to use as freewriting prompts or I imagine the person who wrote them and use that as a starting point for a character.

Look at your collection of lists whenever you're searching for a character to develop or a topic to write about.

One can get just as much exultation
in losing oneself in a little thing as in a big thing.
It is nice to think how one can be recklessly lost in a daisy!
—Anne Morrow Lindbergh, Bring Me a Unicorn

start small

New writers often make the mistake of thinking too big when they're starting out. If they want to write nonfiction, they think: feature article for the *Atlantic Monthly*, *Travel & Leisure*, the *New York Times*. If they're excited about fiction, they decide on the *New Yorker*, *Zoetrope*, or *Glimmer Train*.

I say, start *small*.

Small as in essays and opinion pieces for a not-so-major magazine or a feature for your local paper or regional magazine. These may not seem as glamorous as writing an article for a national magazine, but they're also not as difficult, and if writing magazine features is what you truly want to do, it's still better as a newcomer to start small. Most editors of major magazines agree that the best way to break in is to write fillers, those front-of-the-book, rather short pieces that you can write and submit, or query for. Editors always need these, and besides, feature assignments are often given to writers with a track record, those who either started small with the magazine, or who were first published in other magazines and have clips (photocopied articles) to show.

So, start small. And think short. Start by writing a letter to the editor of a newspaper or magazine. You may laugh, but I started this way. I began doing book reviews (for a magazine no longer in print), then essays, then a feature. That feature led to more features in other magazines.

If you like reading essays, consider writing one. (Whatever you read points to what you should probably be writing, anyway.) The op-ed page of newspapers publishes essays, as do women's magazines and just about every other type of magazine under the sun.

If it's fiction you're interested in, rather than thinking novel, consider the short story. While novels may sell faster than short stories, writing a novel is a huge undertaking, especially if you're just starting out.

Aimee Bender published her collection of short stories *The Girl in the Flammable Skirt* before she attempted to write a novel. She says the short story remains her first love.

"Because the short story is short, the stakes feel lower," says Bender. "You can play, experiment, change voice, anything, and shifting the whole isn't a huge upheaval. A short story reminds me of a song in that way—I'm just trying to capture something elusive and then hold it in my mind and sing it to myself."

Because it takes an average of two to three years to write a first novel, new writers often find their energy waning midway through a book-length project and wind up leaving their manuscript to gather dust. You're more likely to finish a short story and go on to the next, then the next and the next, gaining good experience writing while refining your skills.

Ron Carlson, author of *At the Jim Bridger*, says, "One of the ways I've always spoken about writing short is to compare it to rolling newspapers. When I was a paperboy, and this was for a short period a long time ago, our foreman said, 'Boys, start tight and stay tight.' It was great advice if we were going to get Thursday and Sunday papers in the rubber band. You start tight and that way the whole thing would fit. I see now it makes sense for writers. Start tight, close to your materials. Don't rise to the idea until you've got the rubber band around it."

I'm not saying you should *always* have small goals. Let your goals grow as substantial as you like. What I *am* saying is if you want to write and break into publishing, the best way to do so is to ease in.

After my letters to the editor, poetry, and short fiction, along came essays and *then* feature articles and novels and nonfiction book proposals. But I still love writing short. For three years I wrote a biweekly column for a business/lifestyle magazine that ran 550 words, no more and no less. But that's fine. Writing short fits my attention span, and it has taught me economy of language: How can I say what I want to say in 550 words or less? Writing short can actually be more difficult than writing long rambling pieces.

Jo-Ann Mapson, author of *Goodbye, Earl*, says, "Writing short isn't easy to pull off. I write a column on the writing life for a magazine here in Alaska called *Art Matters*, with a 500- to 600-word limit, and it's tough, trying to say anything of merit and make it hold together or be funny or make a point."

I broke into *Sunset* magazine by first writing short filler pieces for them. After a dozen or so of these, I pitched my *Sunset* editor a feature idea and received an assignment.

So don't think of small as being less. Small can lead to big things.

 ### set your timer

You may love reading hefty novels or biographies and may want to someday write a book. You may even have an idea for one. But for now, write short.

Study the lists you created in the last chapter. Now, put them away and sit quietly. Which entry is still on your mind?

Is there one that, more than the others, pulls you to it, calls out to be written about?

Set the timer for fifteen minutes and start writing. Try not to think too much. Keep the pen moving, as you do when you freewrite.

If you can't seem to come up with anything much to say, pick another item, reset the timer, and start writing. Begin in the middle of things, where the action commences. Do this until an item inspires you to write nonstop for fifteen minutes.

Then, let your piece sit for a few hours or a few days. Pick it up again and read it aloud. Pay attention to rhythm, noticing any places where you need to insert or delete a word or two, or where the story might skip a step.

Notice how "My brother bought his first car when he was a teenager" improves when you get specific: "My brother's first car was a '69 Cadillac Seville." Now you have a precise image.

The same goes for your verbs. First replace passive verbs — *was, is* — with active ones. You may need to rearrange sentence structure. Not: "He was bored with spring break." Rather: "Spring break bored him." See how the energy of the sentence changes?

Moreover, be specific with verb choice. Observe how "She felt sleepy and walked to the kitchen" improves by choosing a better verb and rearranging the sentence: "Half awake, my mother shuffled to the kitchen."

Regardless of how many words you've written, rework the piece so it ends up being about 550 words.

Continue to repeat these steps until you feel your piece is finished and you're ready to show it to someone.

Research is formalized curiosity.
It is poking and prying with a purpose.
—Zora Neale Hurston, Dust Tracks on a Road

regarding research

R esearch can serve various purposes. One is to know what you're writing about. If you want to write a book about the history of clamming or a historical novel that takes place in the 1700s, you will need to research those worlds—through books and other documents—before you start writing.

More books than you may realize are based on research: Laura Hillenbrand's *Seabiscuit*; Dava Sobel's *Longitude*; Chris Bohjalian's *Midwives*; Arthur Golden's *Memoirs of a Geisha*; Margot Livesey's *The Missing World*. Research can be enjoyable, an intellectual type of play. It can take you before people you might never otherwise meet.

Research can also take you away from yourself and serve as a tool of inspiration. You've heard, "Write what you know." Well, what if what you know just doesn't kick-start any ideas? Or you begin writing and you bore yourself?

Tony Eprile, author of *The Persistence of Memory*, who has taught at several universities, finds that many new writers become stuck when writing about themselves and what they know. To get them past the notion they "have nothing else to write about," he often has his students find story ideas through the WPA oral history project from the thirties. He says they become excited by the wealth of experience there is to mine.

His wife, author Judith Schwartz, says, "My bias really is toward immersing oneself intellectually in material outside of one's life. To me, much of contemporary American writing is insular, merely reflecting back and not taking a reader anywhere. As a reader, I love being in the presence of real intelligence, not sound-bite cleverness but intelligence that suffuses the entire work. I like Shirley Hazzard, Graham Greene, Pat Barker. Then again, I am a nerd.

"Yesterday, to research a novel I'm writing, I went to the Throop Museum at the Albany College of Pharmacy, to get a sense of what medicines were like around 1900, and what fabulous stuff! What clever contraptions and [what] great flowery language on the labels! Truth may be stranger than fiction, but there's no reason you can't put it in."

Jodi Picoult, author of *Second Glance*, says an article in the *Burlington Free Press* about local Abenaki protesting against development of burial grounds in Vermont led her to the Internet for further research, and she found information that astounded her about a racial cleansing program in Vermont that was going on pre–World War II.

"I started looking up info on the Abenaki," says Picoult, "and literally fell into the whole eugenics project of the thirties."

Alice McDermott's *A Bigamist's Daughter* originated in research. In graduate school, McDermott wrote a paper on vanity publishing, so when it came time to write a novel, she had all she needed to make her protagonist an editor with a vanity publisher.

Sifting through files on the Internet and books or microfiche at the library can be strangely thrilling. All that information to be gleaned, learned from. But at a certain point, you have to let go.

"Research is addictive," says Dava Sobel. "There comes a time when you must stop and begin writing. A topic like Galileo's daughter... I could have argued to go on and research another five years, even though the book is out there now."

Even when what you are writing is contemporary, you may still need to do some research to fill in gaps. But authors disagree as to when you should research. Writer and therapist Dennis Palumbo says, "Do research later. All you have to know is what's in your heart."

Same goes for Janet Fitch. "I write first and then I research. If I do it the other way, I can't imagine. I can only see what I've seen. Research blocks my creativity. I start to follow the research rather than go down and find what it is I really need to say in this work. In *White Oleander*, I needed to check to see if what I was writing was true. I put up flyers around L.A., looking for people who had been in foster homes as kids. I didn't research the system; I wanted to know what it was like to be an individual *in* the system."

Crime writer and former reporter Laura Lippman says, "One of the things I brought from journalism is what I'll call a healthy disrespect for research. I find that the writers who are really caught up in research tend not to have a journalism background. They take it a lot more seriously than I do. And some of them write absolutely fantastic books, and their books are riveting for all of the knowledge in them. But that's what I wanted to leave behind. I wanted the freedom of writing a plausible story as opposed to writing accurate stories. At the same time I know how to find something out when I need to and can do so quickly and efficiently."

People read to expand their world, to enter into a world they've not known. Research can give you access to worlds you yourself have no firsthand experience with. It can also give you the surprising detail and texture that your work might otherwise lack. Learn to tell the difference between when you should research, when you shouldn't, and when it's time to stop.

❧ set your timer

Take a topic that interests you or one that you love but know little about—the history of the town you live in or one of the city founders, tap dancing, the peanut butter cookie. Do a little research and see where it leads. Surf the Internet, follow threads, and see where you end up.

When you read the newspaper, pay attention to your reaction to stories—especially local stories. In the late nineties, a short piece I read in a newspaper about two local scientists inspired me to write an exposé on Gulf War syndrome.

Does your research inspire you to write an essay, short story, op-ed piece? A novel or nonfiction book? Research is a kind of puzzle. Have fun putting together the pieces. And now set your timer for fifteen minutes and write nonstop about something you found.

tools & rituals

Rituals are a good signal to your
unconscious that it is time to kick in.
—Anne Lamott, BIRD BY BIRD

leave your shoes at the door

Rituals help us change modes. When I enter a Catholic church, I dip my finger in the holy water font and make the sign of the cross on my forehead. It helps me transition to a more spiritual place. Jews light candles on Friday when the sun goes down, signaling the beginning of the Sabbath. Parents shop for clothes with kids at the end of August to get them into school mode. Baking treats puts us in the holiday spirit.

For writers, rituals counteract inertia and trigger the desire to write. When I'm having trouble shifting into writing mode, I make tea or put on instrumental music—Ravi Shankar, Mozart, Debussy, John Coltrane. Music helps me change my frame of mind or transition from busy work, errands, social occasions, or even working on articles to focusing on more creative work. Sometimes I sit somewhere else in the house or go down to Café Zinc to write.

There's no end to what you can do to create your own rituals.

When she needs fresh ideas, mystery writer Barbara Seranella goes for a brisk walk or a swim, or she goes for a drive with rock and roll blasting. She says this works for her because she does it so infrequently.

Chris Bohjalian says he begins by rewriting the last paragraph or two, or even an entire page, from his work the day before. "Hemingway recommended it and I think it's wonderful," says Bohjalian. "You immediately get reacquainted with the story. You are editing and the more you edit, the better the book is going to be. It works as a runway: You literally ramp up to speed to get going.

"And while I don't know precisely what's going to happen in that scene—I don't know what my characters are going to do—before I fall asleep every night, I think about what I'm going to write the next day."

Preparing your work space for the next day is a sort of ritual, too. If your writing space is messy, it's likely you won't be as inspired as you would be if you leave it tidy and neat. If you leave the mess for the next day, you might end up using your entire fifteen minutes of writing time just cleaning up.

Bohjalian, a self-proclaimed obsessive-compulsive, adds: "I do have to have a perfectly feng shui–ordered library; I have to have everything in its place when I start working—there can't be papers on this wonderful 150-year-old pumpkin pine table on which I write."

And for some, a ritual can become a pragmatic reality, as simple and necessary as keeping track of how much writing gets done each day. Tom Paine, author of *The Pearl of Kuwait*, says, "I used to be a person who stumbled around, fiddling with this or that. Then the book became overdue. My editor said, 'You've got to show us something.' So my ritual became checking off the calendar every day. That I wrote five pages that day made me ecstatic."

And for others, there are props. Freelance writer and author Kelly James-Enger says she wears a hat to change mind-sets from nonfiction (which helps her earn the bulk of her living) to fiction. She credits a blue canvas hat with grommets for ventilation ("I've found that writing sex scenes can make you sweaty," says James-Enger) with making it possible for her to finish and sell two novels. "It's goofy, but then again I only wear it to write fiction. With the hat, I don't check e-mail. I don't answer the phone. I don't think of new article ideas. I don't work on current assignments. I simply work on my novel. My hat tells my brain, and my itchy, distractible self, one thing—*it's fiction time, baby*. If my husband asks me something, I yell, 'I'm wearing my hat!' If I have to stop for some reason, to answer the phone or get the door, off comes the hat. When I'm finished with my fiction quota for the day, I take my hat off, where it will be waiting tomorrow."

In India, when you enter an ashram, you slip out of your shoes and leave them, along with the world and all its worries, at the door. While you don't necessarily have to remove your shoes—or wear a hat—to get in the writing mood, you might consider doing something symbolic. Whatever your ritual, in effect you're saying you've taken all your worries about what people will think, all your fears of rejection, all that garbage about how you thought you could never be a writer—you've taken all that useless *stuff* and you've left it outside your door. The ritual can be your entryway into your writing time.

set your timer

Try different rituals before you begin writing to see what works for you. Slip out of your shoes and leave them at the door. Change your clothes or dress up, even. If you're writing fiction, dress in the clothing that your main character would wear. Stay in your jammies and write in bed, or dress as if you are going to a job and go out to a café or restaurant to write. Or write naked (just don't leave the house!).

Put on music, make tea, meditate. Perform a ritual as a way of saying, "This is my show, starting...right...now!" And for fifteen minutes, stay glued to the page.

Pencils must be round. A hexagonal
pencil cuts my fingers after a long day.
—John Steinbeck

writers' utensils

I would much rather shop at an office supply store than a department store. Going to Staples a chore? Never! I'm afraid my son, now nine, has inherited my disease. He calls it "stationery sickness." He has a trillion pens, pencils, markers, notebooks, and tablets. And always needs more—just like me.

For a writer, the proper tools are vital. Writers imbue their tools with all kinds of magical powers. Playwright Athol Fugard starts each new work in a different color ink. When Tony Eprile, author of *The Persistence of Memory*, won his National Endowment for the Arts grant, the first thing he did was spend $275 on a gorgeous green Parker Duofold fountain pen, more than he had ever spent on a gift for himself. He uses it when he's working on fiction and writing longhand and almost never for anything else, such as grading papers.

Kathryn Lance, author of fifty books, says she drafts her nonfiction on computer to do it as fast as possible, but writes fiction by hand. "My special purple pen is a Pentel fine-point RSVP—big and fat and sturdy, for pressing hard. For some reason I press really hard when I write. I love purple ink. I use the same pen for everything and usually have a lot of purple ink stains on the sides of my hands because the ink smears. I use white lined paper, college-ruled. I write on every line, which makes a horrible mess when I revise. Sometimes I use plain tablets, sometimes a spiral notebook (I tend to use notebooks for novels in progress). It's a little bit like sports magic — you know, if the Diamondbacks won when you were wearing a certain red shirt then you have to wear that same shirt whenever you watch a game. So if something got published that I drafted using certain tools, it only made sense to keep using them for the next project."

I advise my students to try writing with a variety of implements to learn how each makes them feel. When I gave them an exercise about a writer's tools, Debra Cross wrote:

> I prefer to switch from one writing tool to another, hoping that I will fool my inner critic — hoping that she'll think it's someone else using my words and not be so, well, critical. I have been known to write with everything from a fountain pen to lipstick liner. I use different colors of ink to evoke emotions and when I use my gold-plated Cross pen, I find that elevated words flow easily. I do not, however, own or use a Mont Blanc — I'm waiting until my words are worthy.

Ron Carlson uses different colored paper for different drafts so "I take the right draft to readings," he says.

T. Jefferson Parker, author of *Cold Pursuit*, says he drafted his fourth novel, *Summer of Fear*, entirely in longhand. "It was a personal book and demanded a personal instrument."

Author Judith Schwartz says, "I love those French Clairefontaine notebooks. I know I'm serious about a project when I devote a Clairefontaine notebook to it. Right now I'm done with a chunk of reading and am ready to start writing, but I don't have a fresh notebook to write in! I'm just keeping it in my head until I get a proper notebook. Am I nuts or what?"

Just as having the right pen can make all the difference in your motivation to write, so can the type of computer you use. Writers spend more time with their computers than with anything — or, in some cases, anyone — else, so we had better like what we use. When I began to dread my daily routine of sitting on the same chair at the same place, with the same view of the wall beyond the PC's big, boxy monitor, I knew it was time to go mobile.

A laptop allows you to work just about anywhere: I've worked on the edge of the field as my son practiced soccer. I've sat on the floor of his room writing as he constructed a K'NEX Rippin' Rocket roller coaster. I work on the bed, at the library, and at the café. A laptop is like a lapdog; it's small enough to accompany you most places. And if you care about aesthetics, laptops can be quite appealing. My laptop is white and pristine and pretty. I don't mind seeing it sitting on the dining-room table. And when I turn it off and close it up, it's barely noticeable against the vintage-patterned tablecloth.

I'm not advising you to buy an expensive computer or pen. What I want is for you to discover which tools work best for you and make you feel as creative as possible. A new pen, notebook, computer, or even a desk might be just the inspiration you need.

Pay attention to your inclinations. And remember to keep it fun.

set your timer

Experiment with different writing instruments. Choose a word or two from your notebook or file, sit down with a legal pad and pen, set the timer for five minutes, and write until you hear the buzzer.

Next, go to your computer, choose a few words, set the timer, and begin freewriting. Don't stop until the timer goes off.

Pick another set of writing utensils: a crayon or eyebrow pencil and a brown paper bag, a manual typewriter, or anything else you can think of. Set the timer for five minutes and write nonstop until the buzzer sounds.

Which feels the best? Which instrument allows you to let go and even forget about what you were using to write? Consider using this mode of writing for the next project you tackle, whether it's a story, essay, poem, or a novel.

Use paper of different sizes. You can even try freewriting with your nondominant hand.

Don't fall into a rut. Every so often, experiment with other modes. Write in a circle, sideways, or diagonally across the page. By keeping your writing methods fresh, you help keep your writing original.

All I needed was a steady table
and a typewriter . . . and a marble-topped bedroom
washstand table made a good place; the dining room
table between meals was also suitable.
—Agatha Christie

where writers work

I t can take time to discover the best work space for you. But beware: The place that works for you one day may not work the next, or might be right for one type of writing and not another.

For a good long time I happily worked away at a chipped white vintage farm table in the corner of the kitchen. (Margaret Atwood wrote *The Edible Woman,* her first novel—and my favorite of hers—at her kitchen table.) I found the table at a flea market and later had a sheet of thick glass cut for the top to prevent further chipping. Beside it, I transformed my dishwasher—working fine, but unused for two years—into a filing cabinet. The pull-out trays hold file folders perfectly.

Although I quite like the table, sitting in the corner of the kitchen began to feel restrictive. Once I bought my laptop, I started experimenting.

I tried working outside on the patio among the plants but—alas—too many distractions. My mind flitted about at the slightest movement, like the hummingbirds that zipped by.

I sometimes work in the bedroom. The light is nicely crepuscular (that word I cribbed from *Underworld* and wrote about in "Harvesting Words"). The high windows face southeast and crank open; they admit ambient light while obscuring views of anything but morning glory vines and bougainvillea.

Lately I mostly work at the dining-room table at one end of the living room (we live in a beach cottage, which makes for snug living). My back is to the wall and there's a view of the street through the plate glass window across the room. I don't expect this spot to work for me forever. What's nice is that with a laptop, it doesn't have to.

If you need intense quiet, you may need a room of your own or office space. When Travis was a toddler, I *thought* I did, so I worked in the studio in back of the house. But the quiet and remove proved to be more disruptive; I constantly wondered what was happening in the house: Who *is* that at the door? Is Travis hungry? Why is the dog barking? It was too distracting. I moved my office back inside.

If you lack space, you may have to work in a room where others in your family spend time. Don't let it stop you. Judy Blunt, a single mother of three and author of the bestselling memoir *Breaking Clean*, says she wrote that book at a desk in the living room after spending the day at her job refinishing floors. "My work area was in the living room, along with a television, front door, telephone, and three busy children bustling about," says Blunt. "I had to learn to focus so incredibly that my children quickly learned they could not come up behind me and touch me on the shoulder or I would explode out of the chair; I was wound down so tight to drive myself into the story, to shut out all extraneous things. They discovered that they could pass their hand between the overhead lightbulb and my computer screen and it would cause a shadow. And that's how they would alert me that they needed my attention."

Tony Eprile built a yurt adjacent to the Vermont home he shares with his wife, Judith Schwartz, and son, Brendan. Once his yurt was habitable, he quickly wrote his book. "Most important for me," says

Eprile, "is one, a place I won't be interrupted; two, a place I go *only* to work. I never take student papers, et cetera, to the yurt. The only thing I do there is my own writing. When I get there, I know that's what I'm there to do."

It's hardly news that many writers swear by cafés; Natalie Goldberg, author of *Writing Down the Bones*, has always written in cafés. Cafés have become one of the most popular places to write. Literary agent Laurie Fox says she wrote the entire first draft of her novel, *My Sister from the Black Lagoon*, at coffeehouses in Berkeley, a writer's town with more than seventy cafés (excluding Starbucks) to choose from. She chose her work places "for the lighting, the lack of general noise, the perch—I like to be flat against the wall—and the fact that the music was instrumental and, *oh!* the coffee has to be good and strong.

"I don't know if this is common to other writers," Fox says, "but the moment my laptop lights up, it has my attention and holds me captive. I am glued to the screen. Typically, I love to people-watch, but not when the laptop beckons."

Poet Gerald Stern goes for more common environs. "Across the river in New Hope, Pennsylvania, is a McDonald's. I read the *Philadelphia Inquirer* because it's not as challenging as the *New York Times* and it has more delightful gossip. Then I write some lines down. Sometimes they work, sometimes they don't."

Writing in bed has its advantages. Colette wrote by the light of a blue lamp while she sat up in bed between blue sheets. When Fox came down with fibromyalgia, a close cousin to chronic fatigue syndrome, she gave up writing in cafés and started writing in bed, too. She says she wrote much of her latest novel, *The Lost Girls*, sitting propped up against pillows.

Former *Ladies' Home Journal* editor and author of ten books, Sondra Forsyth, also works in bed. She says, "I do my very best work in bed, still in my jammies, propped up with a backrest and tapping out articles, queries, book chapters, on my laptop. I left my office job precisely so I wouldn't have to dress for success. Now I never get gorgeous until late in the afternoon before I go take a predinner ballet class. Now *that's* a lifestyle to love!"

There are also libraries, public writing places like The Writers Room in New York City, and the houses or apartments of friends while they're at work or on vacation. Find a venue that fits your life.

Kevin Garrison, an airline captain and a journalist who has produced more than 850 articles, says, "I've written articles while sitting in the captain's seat as my 777 flew over the Arctic Circle. I've written on my laptop while sitting on the jump seat in a Paris rainstorm as we approached Orly. I've done rewrites of material while holding over Scotland waiting for Gatwick to open up. I usually stay away from writing about aviation stuff as I fly and I never write when I'm actually at the controls. I normally write my newspaper humor column or work on book projects. Not because I wouldn't be able to write and fly at the same time (anybody that has read my stuff will testify that it doesn't take *that* much thought) but because my laptop doesn't fit between my ample stomach and the control column. When I'm deadheading—riding in the passenger cabin to be relocated to a place where I can resume flying the airplane—or when I was the relief pilot flying international in the jump seat, is when I do my airborne writing. Writing in a plane is far better than writing on the ground because I get paid to do both at the same time."

The Writer's Desk is a lovely book of photographs by Jill Krementz that shows writers in a range of writing places and positions. Rita Dove and Saul Bellow stand at tall writing desks working. Toni Morrison sits on the sofa with a legal pad and pen. Joan Didion and the late E. B. White occupy rooms empty of most everything but typewriters.

Wherever you work, let it be a place you enjoy. "Like Archimedes, I do my best thinking in the bath," says Cleo Paskal, travel columnist for Canada's *National Post* and Emmy Award–winning TV writer. "I recently judged a major literary competition and went through 180 manuscripts in two soaking sessions. But I have no favorite place to write-work. I once got a lot of writing done in a hotel room in Christchurch. Otherwise, I usually end up at my kitchen table, within easy reach of comfort food. It gives me buoyancy in the bath."

Just as writing is a process of discovery, so is finding the best work space for you. You will find out how and when you work best by trying out different methods. Writers write everywhere, and some of the best writers write with the most meager of accoutrements.

⟨image⟩ set your timer

Try altering your routine to see what happens.

Every day for a week spend fifteen minutes writing in a different location. Write at a desk, on the couch, on the bathroom floor, at the park, at a restaurant, or on a bus. Write sitting on a chair, standing up, lying down. Write in bright light, low light, blue light. Experiment. See what works for you. In the meantime, you will have collected pages. And that is a very good thing.

Walking is almost an ambulation of the mind.
—Gretel Ehrlich, ISLANDS, THE UNIVERSE, HOME

walk! refresh! have fun!

We all have days when no matter how much we think we may want to write, nothing comes—at least nothing worth writing, and at least not right away. Or it's impossible to focus because of the clutter everywhere: in the house, in your e-mail in-box, on your desk, and in your brain. Perhaps you've simply been sitting too long and need to move before one more interesting thought comes to you.

Judith Handelsman-Smith, author of *Growing Myself: A Spiritual Journey Through Gardening*, says that over the years, she's learned that as a writer, she needs to spend a lot of time ruminating. "In fact, there's an aspect of writing that I call back-burnering," she says. "It's a visceral process in which you're writing without your conscious knowledge. I go out in the garden and spend time with my plants. I meditate. I used to think you had to sit there six or ten hours a day or you weren't a real writer, but that's not true. When I'm feeling burned out, I don't force myself."

For travel writer Arline Zatz, kayaking clears her head. "When sitting in front of the computer drains my brain and I can no longer think, I load my kayak on top of my car and head for quiet water. As I paddle along, I somehow am able to think of the first few paragraphs of a new feature or am able to come up with an ending. So as not to forget these thoughts, I have a voice-activated tape recorder (minicassette) in my life jacket top pocket."

There is a long tradition of writers walking to let the mind wander, to take it all in, to clear the cobwebs. Dava Sobel, author of *Galileo's Daughter*, says walking works wonders for her. "I live in a place where it's very nice to walk," she says. "Two miles from here is a very nice view. The walk is four miles. Whenever I'm working on something, I take that walk every day. And that will often make things fall into place for me."

One summer day in late July when I was installed in my office across the courtyard from the house, I realized I hadn't focused for at least fifteen minutes. My mind was adrift and my body was twitchy. Muscles are a bit like kittens: Ignore them and they insist on your attention. Why fight it? My work clothes that day were also my walking attire—black leggings and an oversized gray T-shirt imprinted with the words YOU DON'T KNOW ME. So I locked the studio door and went for a walk.

Walking invites serendipity, internal and external. I was reminded of this when I saw a candy-apple red Austin Healy bug-eyed Sprite. A slew of memories swept in. I was sixteen and my first big boyfriend, Bill Bair, was teaching me how to drive in his white Sprite. How that poor car bucked about the Gwynedd Manor parking lot.

It was always night when Bill let me drive. As I walked, memories of the two years we dated came flooding back: his parents, their copper-colored '68 Mustang, his dog named Cindy, the faux living room we created in his parents' basement; the trees Bill planted in my parents' yard; the ninth-grade prom, me wearing a white lace dress and being named first runner-up to the prom queen Judy Moyer. I could still see the teacher's elfin face.

All this because of that candy-apple red Austin Healy Sprite.

I squinted from the sunlight, remembering something an older woman who is a friend of mine recently said: "I don't regret having regrets. I only wished they had come sooner." A story percolated and I didn't want to regret not writing it.

Obviously the walk made no noticeable change in my physique. Yet something had happened on the inside. I went into the studio and reached for paper and pen. That red sports car was calling to me.

There are also times when you need to follow impulses to have fun, or simply do nothing. It was the middle of the day in July as I sat in the dim light of our bedroom with my gleaming white laptop. Books and pages stretched across the quilt. Our kitty, Jo-Jo, three months old, lay on my table of contents. He knew I wanted to look at it, I'm certain, because he seemed to have no intention of moving. Then he gave his paw a contemplative lick, got up, and moved a few feet over to the back of my laptop. He pulled his paws up under him and settled into a light nap.

We are so busy, we women—and men. So much to do, so little time. But I felt myself decelerate into slow-down mode. I wanted to take the time to play with my boy, to water the garden, to follow the lead of my lazy kitten. On certain days, no matter what my intentions may be, I just need to give in to my impulses.

So, take a break! Don't beat up on yourself. Have fun. Relax. A writer has to make time in her life for games of solitaire, baking oatmeal cookies, going to the beach, hiking in the woods, watching the sunset, sitting by the pool with a tall cool drink, reading a good book—or a trashy one—paging through catalogs, going to the mall. Even cleaning the grout has its place. Whatever you enjoy, however odd, now's the time.

Our brains occasionally act like computers in freak-out mode. The only way to get them working again is to reboot. Sometimes you must even unplug the contraption and wait awhile. Then when you turn it back on, *voilà!*

When I'm in this no-words-available mood or just so distracted I don't even want to sit still, taking a half hour or an hour or three to do nothing can work wonders. Meditate, do Pilates, stretch, walk. My student Jess Beauchaine says napping for a half hour works for her, and if she's at work and can't nap, she'll find a place to sit—outside if the weather is good—where she can stare into the sky or at the ground and let her thoughts fall away.

It's been said, if you want to change your writing, change your life. Eat persimmons at midnight, play poker with your three-year-old, make fortune cookies stuffed with outrageous fortunes, do freewriting with your mother.

Remember, it's good to get up every so often, anyway. Sitting for more than twenty or thirty minutes at a time compresses the disks in the vertebrae and brings on early arthritis. Take care of your health. Move around. Go for walks. Enjoy your life.

set your timer

Get out of your writing space and go for a walk. Better to go alone, but if you want to walk with someone, agree not to talk; your task is to observe. Young children in strollers are great companions because they love the movement and are happy watching their surroundings (until they become unhappy and begin screaming).

Pay attention to the light, smells, sounds, houses, and cars. What do things look like? Do any memories come forth? Sometimes you have to do something like get outside for the muse to find you. Don't make the mistake of waiting for her to visit; she's so very busy these days.

When you return home, pour a cool glass of water, do some stretches, then sit down and set the timer. Write down everything you remember about your walk. Write about the weather and the landscape. Write specifics—recall how the pink gladiolas you saw growing in your neighbor's garden reminded you of a tutu you once wore in a ballet recital in the first grade, describe the sounds you heard, explain what the people, animals, and bugs you saw were doing. Include that contingent of ants marching somewhere and don't forget the hummingbird that whizzed by in a blur.

What else did you observe? Who did you pass on the street and did you have any sort of encounter, however brief? Did anything remind you of another time in your life?

Describe in minute detail your walk so that someone who wasn't with you and doesn't live in your town would feel as if she were there. Write it for yourself, too, so that years from now, when you reread it, you will once again smell the fragrant pine trees in the misty morning.

Or stay home and have fun. (You know best what you need.) You can even invite some friends over and play writing games. Remember that game you played as a child where one person whispered a sentence or phrase into the ear of the person beside her and by the time it reached the last child, what started out as "spaghetti and meatballs" became "Mrs. Hoogenschmidt's wiener dog"?

This is similar, only you do it with writing. The bigger the group the better. Everyone takes a sheet of paper, writes down a sentence, and passes it to the left. You then write a line or phrase on the paper you've been handed. You keep it going until the page is filled. When everyone receives their own paper back, take turns reading them aloud.

Write a story only using words with one syllable.

Go to the kitchen cabinet and look at labels and use them as prompts. Sit on a raft in the pool and write about life as a fish or a mermaid. Take a cliché, such as "Don't beat up on yourself," and go with it. Write from the point of view of your pet: What's it like to be a cockatiel riding your owner's shoulder as she moves down the street or to be a dog at the end of a leash?

Again, have fun with writing and have fun with your life.

The writer is either a practicing recluse
or a delinquent, guilt-ridden one—or both. Usually both.
—Susan Sontag

motel motivation

I love hotels, motels, resorts, guest ranches, and inns. I love anywhere that is anonymous, temporary, and has few distractions. I love going to these places with a suitcase full of clothes—more than I will ever wear—and a bagful of books, paper, and pens. As much as I like our home, leaving it behind for a place that has a front desk, big white towels, and wrapped soap in a dish sparks my imagination.

The first time I took advantage of motel motivation, I was finishing up a collection of short stories for my senior project in college. I was going through a hard time with my painter boyfriend, and I needed to get away by myself. I loaded my green '68 Pontiac Tempest, a car that had belonged to my mother, with a suitcase full of clothes, stories, and notebooks, and drove 150 miles from Vermont to Woodstock, New York. I checked into a Holiday Inn and did little but write and read. When my three days were over, I left with revised stories, a lighter heart, and a solid resolve to end the relationship with my boyfriend.

Writing in hotels and motels is a pleasure. It's the perfect way to escape distractions, unless TV is a serious temptation for you. If it is, you can always find an inn without a TV in every room. My friends Jess, Liz, Kerry, and I holed up for a weekend at the Korakia Pensione in Palm Springs (which has no TVs) and held our own private artists' colony.

A motel with a restaurant or a nearby café can be wonderful, too, because it allows you to become a writing machine, leaving your work only for meals. Or if your family is with you, the café can be your retreat, the perfect place to get in writing time. I've also gotten work done while sitting by the pool, or I'll send Brian and Travis off to swim while I remain sequestered in the room.

When you travel with your family, you may not get the volume of work done that you would if you were alone, but you can still do something while recharging. If nothing else, you can gather your thoughts, write down ideas, observe the people around you, and reflect on experiences. Working doesn't always mean putting words on paper.

Jennifer Lawler, author of *Dojo Wisdom for Writers: 100 Simple Ways to Become a More Inspired, Successful, and Fearless Writer*, says that a few years ago, when she was still married and had a book deadline she was lagging on, she checked into a hotel thirty miles from her home.

"I wasn't making enough progress on my book, what with being interrupted all the time with my daughter Jessica's needs. And my husband would complain if I worked while he was home (shouldn't shock anyone that the conflict over my work was a big factor in our divorce!). I read about a woman with five or six kids who used to just go to a hotel for a week at a time and write her books. She'd get a draft done in a week and then come home and polish it up while doing all the ordinary 'housewife' chores. I mentioned this story to my husband (repeatedly) and finally said I wanted to try to get this book done. He agreed to care for our daughter [for] one weekend while I went away. I got a draft done, felt totally luxurious for a while, and came home refreshed and energized. I'd recommend it in a minute for someone trying to get a tough job done. But don't go anywhere too fun, and it's best to try someplace not far from home."

Daylle Deanna Schwartz, the author of eight books, including *All Men Are Jerks until Proven Otherwise*, says she's always on the lookout for somewhere she can go for at least four days to write.

"When I did a speaking tour of Texas, I stayed a few extra days to write. My hotel had a pool that no one used so I sat on a chaise lounge with my laptop for hours. Two summers ago I went to a B&B in Vermont for five days of uninterrupted writing on their gorgeous deck. In June I went to Bryce Canyon and spent every day writing till late afternoon, at which time I'd take a long hike, and then [go] back to writing."

set your timer

When you're feeling stuck, or just plain uninspired, check out of your routine and check in somewhere: no phone calls to return, no mail to open, no newspapers demanding your attention. Just make sure you turn off your cell phone and you don't start fussing with e-mail. Enjoy yourself with your paper and pen or laptop—and your writing.

If it doesn't feel right to go away without your partner, or your kids, bring them along and lay down the ground rules: where and when you're going to write, if and when the TV is to be off.

While away, if you're at a loss for what to write, record details of what you see. Sit in a restaurant or coffee shop and eavesdrop on conversations. Catch a snippet of overheard dialogue and continue the conversation in your writing. Allow a story to emerge. Consider the waitress. What sorts of stories do you think she has? Begin with the name on her badge. Get your partner—or child—to do freewriting with you. You might find that he or she is a writer in disguise.

The important thing is to keep writing. You could always begin with the line, "I love motels..."

So the point of my keeping a notebook has never been,
nor is it now, to have an accurate factual record of what I have
been doing or thinking . . . Perhaps it never did snow that August in
Vermont; perhaps there never were flurries in the night wind, and maybe
no one else felt the ground hardening and summer already dead even as
we pretended to bask in it, but that was how it felt to me, and it
might as well have snowed, could have snowed, did snow.
—Joan Didion

napkins, notebooks, and journals

I have dozens of notebooks filled with snippets of overheard dialogue, details about people and landscapes, words I like and wish to remember, ideas I want to keep. I try to keep paper everywhere: in the car and the bathroom, in purses and tote bags. You never know when you will want to write something down. When I don't have a tablet nearby, I use whatever's available: smooth bark from a eucalyptus tree, a gum wrapper, tissue, napkin, newspaper, the back of a receipt.

And I can't seem to throw any of my notebooks away. Even though at times I'm sure I should, before my son grows older and can read my jangled, hurried scrawl and learns that his mother was a wild child in her younger days, a tad fickle and too in love with love. Still, every so often I do look through my notebooks and find a line or image to use in a current work. The words I've written in my notebooks conjure up times, places, people. I don't trust my memory, no matter how vivid the moment or detail. Certainly it's difficult to remember exact nuances without writing them down.

When one of my best friends, Kerry Rutherford, turned forty, we flew to San Francisco to celebrate. Our first night there we sat on stools at a bar in a jazz club near our hotel. I so wanted to remember the details that I knew would escape me if I didn't write them down. I grabbed a couple of napkins and began writing:

> Blue Curaçao, root beer schnapps, crème de menthe, Frangelico, Grappa Piave: "The drink of Julius Caesar," says David, the black bartender. Sambuca. Blue neon. Something so soothing about blue neon, like swimming pools at night in the desert. A framed print of a baby blue packet of Gauloises, the word "caporal" beneath it and a logo of a helmet with wings.
>
> A Japanese girl with short wavy hair that looks more like a wig than her own hair goes up to the stage and the jazz band backs her as she sings the theme song from *Black Orpheus*. But she sings off-key, Yoko Ono–like, and ruins the mood.
>
> At the other end of the bar stands a man in a black turtleneck sweater. His face is blank, expressionless. It masks interest in anything or anyone around him. The Japanese girl asks him to dance. He smiles shyly as he turns her down. He wears jeans and just-do-it Nikes. His eyebrows sweep upward as if he's mildly astonished. We learn his name is Maximilliano.

Many writers won't go anywhere without a notebook. You never know when something will hit and you will need to write it down. Jayne Anne Phillips, author of *Black Tickets* and *MotherKind*, says, "That little italicized section in *Shelter* that starts out about the sky: 'The sky burned white to blond to powder blue,' that was a paragraph in my notebook maybe fifteen years before the book was written, and I knew it was a book about these girls at camp, and that's all I knew.

I have pieces of books in my notebooks that I do end up making books to go with them."

Susanna Moore, author of *In the Cut* and *The Whiteness of Bones*, says, "There's something that happens when you're in the grip of the work, a moment in which almost everything you are seeing, feeling, smelling, experiencing, goes into the work. During that period, which is quite thrilling, you're always scribbling something into your notebook."

Don't rely on your memory. It's faulty. These moments can be as fleeting as dreams and just as hard to remember the next day.

For instance, last night as I lay in bed, a thought came to me. *Write about Kerry's and my visit to San Francisco in the chapter on keeping a notebook.* But there were no tablets beside the bed or on the shelf of my night table, and I was falling asleep and didn't want to turn the light back on.

Ah, you'll remember in the morning. Then my better self said, *Oh, no, you won't.* I turned on my lamp, pulled open the drawer, and under my beading board found a yellow Post-It note on which I scribbled my thoughts. Such a simple note, you'd think I'd remember in the morning. But I know myself well enough to know I wouldn't. Better to have to work my way back to sleep than to pass up a good idea.

Earlier I suggested that for freewriting, you might use a cheap notebook so you can let loose and be as wordy and rambling as you like.

Journals are just the opposite. Journals tend to be for an audience, even if that audience is only you years from now. You take more care in choosing a journal and tend to be more deliberate with what you write on its pages. I choose journals I like the look and feel of and that have paper—usually unlined—with an appealing texture.

When Mary Morris, travel memoirist and novelist, came on *Writers on Writing*, she talked about the extensive journals she keeps and how they help her when she sits down to write.

"A lot of the scenes in *Angels and Aliens* were in my journals, almost exactly as they happened," she said. "I spend a lot of time roughing things out in my journals. Sometimes I open them up and work is already there, very much like an artist would use a sketchbook."

Writing is like passing messages, if you think about it. When you write, you're having a conversation with another person, a reader — even if that reader is you. One way to get a head start in writing or to do something gratifying with writing is to exchange journal entries with someone you live with, ideally your spouse or significant other if you're comfortable, although you can also do it with a close friend.

Shortly after Brian moved in, we began keeping a journal together. He often worked late into the night playing music. If I wasn't out with him, I was often sleeping by the time he came home, so I would write in our journal before I went to bed and leave it for him to read when he returned home. He'd respond and leave it out for me to read in the morning.

We don't write in it as much as we used to — his gigs usually don't keep him out as late as they once did — but we still fill a book every two years. We write about what Travis said or did. We recall random thoughts and we continue discussions interrupted by daily life. Or we write reminders of love that sometimes include line drawings. We think of it as a literary album of our secret world.

We have also kept a journal for Travis since he was born. It is addressed to him, as in, "Travis, today you went for your first walk in the garden..." In it we tell him things about himself and his life: funny or profound things he said or did, his vocabulary — spelled phonetically — when he was two. On one of the pages I glued a sprig of rosemary from the garden that I broke off and held to his nose on one of our first jaunts around the yard when he was just a week or so old. On the opposite page I wrote about his reaction. Some entries are entirely dialogue.

Journals can be a legacy you leave for those you love. They are also like a savings account; the details you've recorded — what something looked like, smelled like, what someone said — might be just what you need for a future piece of work or for inspiration. When you're stuck for what to write, you can always open your journal and find something to expand on.

set your timer

Observing and learning to describe the little things, the minute and mundane details of life, will help you bring color and life to your other writing. Listening to and recording choice tidbits of what people say—those sentences that make you lean in, wanting to hear more—will help you write dialogue.

No writer should be without notebooks and a journal, so make a small investment in your future. Go to an office supply store, stationery store, or a bookstore and stock up. Buy little notebooks easily carried in your purse or pocket, and choose a journal with a beautiful cover. Station it somewhere in the home where it's accessible enough but not so public that when people stop by to visit, they pick it up and read. Moleskin journals are a personal favorite.

Take down notes when you notice something you want to be sure to remember, and write in your journal when you're moved to do so. Be loose with when you write in it. Do it when you're inspired, not because you feel obligated. At restaurants write down what people say. Write down observations, startling imagery, details about the interiors of buildings. As you fall asleep, jot down that thing you're sure you'll remember in the morning but won't.

If you're keeping a journal for a child, listen for those memorable things he or she says and does, favorite songs, foods, words, activities. This journal will give you and your child memories you would likely forget had you not written them down.

Set the timer for fifteen minutes and begin writing to someone who truly matters to you, maybe your lover or your child, about that person's day, or yours, or whatever you've been dwelling on. Revel in the details. Don't settle for, "Today you said something really cute." Be more specific: "Today you said that when you grow up and buy a car, if you have any money left over, you're either going to have flames painted along its sides or you'll have it painted blue with pink polka dots. (Nine years old)."

Besides all else, you are creating a lifelong memento unlike any other.

Writing more and more to the sound of music,
writing more and more like music. Sitting in my studio
tonight, playing record after record, writing, music a stimulant
of the highest order, far more potent than wine.
—Anaïs Nin

teaching your pen to listen

Rainstorms are unusual here in Southern California, but I welcome them with outstretched arms. I'm from back East; I love rain and all forms of precipitation, even hail. The winter when Travis was three, the infamous El Niño brought so much rain. Travis begged to go outside, so I dressed him in a big parka and cowboy boots, and he stood on the front porch and repeatedly filled a plastic bag with rainwater, threw it, and watched it splat on the sidewalk. The big *bloosh!* sound as it hit made him shriek and made me listen.

As I sat on the other side of the screen door watching him, I also listened to the rain. *What does it sound like?* Writers are forever making what something is into something else, looking for similes, metaphors. When I shut my eyes I heard the pop and crackle, the *hiss*, and I was transported back to the Blue Spruce Diner on the outskirts of Lansdale, Pennsylvania, where, at fifteen, I worked as a waitress: Oil sizzled on the gigantic griddle as Shorty, the owner, no taller than me, who had a huge, shiny bald head, square white teeth, and a diamond ring stuck on his stubby pinkie, flipped burgers. "See You in September" and "Red Rubber Ball" played on the jukebox, providing the sound track as rice pudding gurgled in a vast aluminum pot and naked russet potatoes waited on the wooden block to be sliced, pared, or chopped.

Sound is so important to creative writing. Think of the sounds you hear that you include in your work and the similes you use to describe what things *sound* like: "As she walked up the alley, her polyester workout pants sounded like windshield wipers swishing back and forth." Cadence, onomatopoeia, the poetry of language are all so important. Learn all that you can about how to bring sound into your work.

Music ushers forth memories. It marks moments: falling in love, breaking up, weddings, rocking the baby to sleep. It brings back darker times, too. Whenever I hear "Ave Maria," no matter where I am, inside my head it is that week between Christmas and New Year's, 2001, and I am back in Lansdale, Pennsylvania, at my mother's funeral, and we are leaving the church, passing beneath a wall of stained glass windows as the choir belts out that song.

My earliest recollection of music is listening to "How Much Is That Doggie in the Window?" by Peggy Lee in the living room of our house on Bellmeade Drive in Altoona, Pennsylvania.

Sounds propel me forward in time, too. Minimalist music, Gregorian chants, and classical music scrub my mind clean and make me more contemplative.

Equally important is what you listen to *when* you work. Fleetwood Mac, Jackson Browne, and Bob Dylan accompanied my hermit phase in Vermont, when I wrote in the kitchen on a wobbly card table that teetered under the weight of my industrial-sized Olivetti Underwood. When I wasn't writing, I developed film and printed black-and-white pictures in my closet darkroom, singing along to *Blood on the Tracks* and wearing out my favorite albums.

Music therapists say that music affects the healing process, and that when you're ill or disturbed or just trying to get creative work done, there are specific types of music you should listen to. Jazz and various classical composers, especially Mozart and Bach, are said to promote creativity. It's the same with writing; depending on what you are working on, different music helps, or hinders.

Student Jordan Finkler always writes to music. "Classical music and mostly adagios, no lyrics," he says. "Lately it's the Haydn cello concerto—the cello solo. I react like a Pavlovian dog."

Music can also act as a cue. Taylor Smith, author of *Liar's Market*, says she often chooses a particular CD—usually something classical—and plays it over and over until she's in what she calls "the zone." She says, "Then, when I start back the next day, I put it on again to get carried quickly back to that place, tricking myself into a quick focus."

As author Don Stanwood says, "Fiction needs a kind of score." It's true. Nothing can put you in a particular mood faster than music.

set your timer

What is your earliest musical memory? Is there a song that stands out from when you were sixteen? Who were you with? What were you doing? What about when you were twenty-one? Thirty-three? Forty? What played at your wedding or when your child was born? For fifteen minutes, write.

Experiment with music. Play different types of music and write. How does what you listen to affect what you write?

Put on music you like, set the timer for fifteen minutes, and write whatever comes through. Don't try to make it into something else. Not yet, anyway. Let the music take you and your writing with it, and see what happens.

Work with similes, as well. Set the timer for fifteen minutes and start with what you hear. Let it lead you. What does what you hear remind you of? What does the rain sound like to you? What do the tires moving past your house sound like? The whistle of the teakettle? Pay attention to sounds as you sit and write, as you walk, as you do what you do, and bring those sounds into your writing.

The writer must be willing, above everything
else, to take chances, to risk making a fool of himself—
or even to risk revealing the fact that he is a fool.
—Jessamyn West, To See the Dream

writers groups

These days writers groups are easy to find, but the trick is finding the one that's right for you. Go online, enter the words "writers groups" in any search engine, and you'll come up with more links than you'll ever have time to research. Just about every city of any size has at least one group where writers get together, usually on a regular basis, to support each other and critique one another's work. Many writers can't do without them.

Author Martin J. Smith finds writers groups invaluable as "frontline" critics. He says, "They offer feedback at a point when it's very easy to change the story to overcome perceived problems. I like to think the book has been pre-edited when I turn it in. I never let the group write the book; I'm the one with the vision. But the early input makes it possible to pick and choose ideas that will improve the story. The rest I can disregard with no hard feelings."

A photography critique group taught me just how much another's perspective is necessary to balance out my own. During a photo critique in college, we took turns hanging our black-and-white prints for everyone to see and comment on. One day I put up prints I thought were pretty good—still lifes of the Vermont landscape, stark black tree limbs against a flat winter sky. Safe images. My other photos lay in a pile on the floor.

Our instructor, Jeff Weiss, sauntered along the wall where the photos hung. He stopped, looked at one, said, "Hmm," and moved on to the next. He peered down at my pile of discards. "What's this?"

I started to say, "Oh, they're just—" but before I could finish, he picked them up and rifled through them. They were portraits of my mother. I had wanted to do nudes of her—I was in my nude phase, common to all art students—but my mother, in her fifties at the time, wouldn't allow it. Instead, she offered to choose her own getup: black sunglasses, a black bra, black panty hose, and high-heeled sandals.

In one shot, she posed with her leg in the refrigerator, one high-heeled foot propped beside pristine white eggs. In another, she sat on the counter smoking a Pall Mall, my brother's high school graduation photo slipped under her bra strap and a snapshot of her new husband, George, tucked into the waistband of her panty hose. These shots were fun, but to me, they were simply pictures that documented that rare summer in the seventies when my mother and I were best friends.

Jeff started replacing the stark landscape photos with the shots of Mom. They were my best so far, he said. They were unique, peculiar to my experience. He said they possessed soul. This last comment I savored. It has stayed with me, compelling me to continue to take risks with my art, to resist playing it safe.

Over the years I've also remembered that my own opinion of my work isn't always to be trusted. Innumerable times I've gone to my writing critique group with a chapter I hate and they've loved it, or I've brought one I love, and *they* think it stinks. You can't always see your own work the way it needs to be seen; you're too close.

Many professional writers have small writing groups they've been in for years, while others can't bear the group process and have one or two readers they trust.

In groups, you need to learn to listen thoughtfully to others' reactions. Are they all saying the same thing or voicing different concerns? When everyone reaches a consensus that something is working or not working, pay attention. And how are they reacting nonverbally? Do you hear paper shuffling, throats clearing? Or are they quiet and attentive? Do they laugh, cry?

Even in good groups, you've got to learn to judge who's speaking. Know critics' preferences in reading and writing. Are they well-read in your genre? Consider where they're coming from and how that might influence their response to your work. If you're a literary writer and the group member who is critiquing you only reads mysteries or romances, you'll have to decide what to listen to and what to let roll off your back. You also have to be careful not to write for the group and not to be influenced by members' preferences.

Margot Livesey, author of *The Missing World*, says, "You have to be both stubborn and open to other people's opinions. And listen to yourself *as well* as to other people."

Paying attention to her group's reactions to her work helped mystery author Barbara Seranella amp up her writing. She says, "I was tired of going to my writing group, reading my work, and hearing, 'That's nice,' or 'That's competent.' I wanted to knock their socks off; I wanted to silence the crowd."

Finding a group can be tricky. If you're new to writing, the best way is to take a class at a college or university. Talk to the instructor; see if she has a group you might join or whether she would consider putting a group together. Two of the critique groups I hold in my home evolved from university classes I taught.

Groups also form, sans instructor, from college extension classes. Check bulletin boards at libraries and bookstores for groups. The upside is that more-informal peer groups can feel less like a class and are free. The downside is that without a facilitator, groups often fall apart or become a free-for-all.

Attend readings, book signings, writers' conferences, and summer workshops, and network with other writers. Stay away from online critique groups made up of people you don't know. These groups often turn nasty because you inevitably run into someone with an agenda the size of Alaska. Not that you won't encounter someone in a hometown group that spoils it for everyone; too often there is one hunk of Limburger on a platter of fragrant cheeses. I ran into this problem in the first group I got involved with when I moved to Orange County from San Francisco. I brought a novel in progress with black characters. One member said, "I don't like black people so I don't have anything to say." I left the group not long thereafter.

Even in the best of groups, some members can be harsh when critiquing one another's work. Don't be deterred by this. Even critiques that make you wince can be useful if they are coming from the right place. The main thing is to be in a group in which members truly want each other to be successful and are able to critique your work with a view to what you're trying to do, not what they would have you do.

set your timer

Before you throw away those scenes you're sure are lousy, show them to your writing group. If you don't yet have readers, ask a friend who reads — the most blunt person you know is a good choice — to look over your work. Ask her to be brutally honest. While she may have gotten on your nerves when you needed a sensitive soul to understand what you were going through, she will be invaluable when you need a frontline critic, as Smith put it.

If you want a group and can't find one, consider putting one together yourself. Assign three writers a session (in my workshops, prior to class, we privately review up to twelve double-spaced pages from each of the three writers so we have more class time for critiquing), and create a critique guideline form: what works, what doesn't work, what do you like, what more do you need from the writing, which sentences or sections work especially well, and nitpicks (things that bug you, such as the repetition of a certain word, the lack of commas, or too many exclamation points). Set a timer and, depending on the size of the group, give everyone two to three minutes to respond. When someone is critiquing, no one else is allowed to talk. And the writer cannot say a word until everyone has taken a turn. Ultimately, the group should help, not hinder, your writing and creativity.

mining
your life

expose yourself

The more difficult your childhood, the more misunderstood you were, the more likely it is that you will become a writer. Writing is a way of pulling back, making sense, and surviving. While not all writing is about healing—that's not primarily why creative writers write—some of it is. Writing is sometimes the only way you can make sense of why your parents argued or why a certain friend just disappeared from your life or how you reacted when your husband or wife or significant other fell in love with someone online.

Fortunately, we writers have a chance to rewrite life the way we imagine it might have been or would have liked it to be. When Natalie Goldberg came on my show, she said something that continues to resonate for me: "Writers live twice." How true. Some of our best writers take their own experiences and transform them into art. The father's health problems in *The Corrections* echoed Jonathan Franzen's own father's challenges. In her lovely memoir, *Slow Motion*, Dani Shapiro wrote about one of her most trying years when her parents were in a car accident and she was involved with a married man. In *Meditations from a Movable Chair*, Andre Dubus wrote movingly about being Catholic and about being confined to a wheelchair.

Even when writers of fiction make it all up, their lives can't help but find their way into their work. Chris Bohjalian is the author of a half dozen novels, including *Midwives* and *The Buffalo Soldier*, which revolves around a foster child. "There are bits of autobiographic minutiae scattered throughout this novel, as there are in all of my books," he says. "I was never a foster child but we moved a lot when I was growing up. I counted it up for my daughter: I went to eight different public schools."

Sometimes it's those things you would never in your right mind write about that are actually the things that you *should* write about. They may not seem all that interesting to you—because you lived through them and know them all too well—or you may just feel they are too personal and nobody else will ever relate. You may also worry about exposing too much or being too offbeat. What if you go too far? You might well be kicked out of the parent-faculty organization at your child's school, or worse.

Author Diana Wagman encountered trouble after her first novel, *Skin Deep*, came out. A preschool parent read it and refused to allow her daughter to continue playing with Wagman's daughter. Wagman says her main character, Martha, was unlike mothers in most books, in that she disliked her own daughter. "It made the preschool parent uncomfortable," says Wagman. "My editor had me scale it back a little, but just a little. It was a very important part of the story and very necessary to her character. I think this parent was afraid of what I might say. I tried to tell her it was fiction! But she didn't get it."

The authors I most admire put it all out there for readers to do with what they will. These authors know there is power in the darkness they've lived through or have seen through the eyes of others and they're willing to harness that power and stream it into words.

I had been writing the "Women's Business" column for a regional Southern California business lifestyle magazine going on two months when my mother was hospitalized. It was clear she would never return to her home. I could think about nothing else. So when I started my column, writing about my mother was all I could do. Here's the beginning:

> Last week a Pennsylvania police officer phoned me. He had just returned from my mother's home where he found her lying facedown in her front yard. She fell while searching for her dog that had died three weeks previous. The officer said she couldn't get up on her own, and he took her to the hospital where she underwent testing.
>
> When the officer and I hung up, my mind raced. This is the call everyone with an aging parent dreads. And it's not one you can prepare for. The worry about my mother's well-being and the guilt over moving to California in 1979 bombarded me: Good Italian daughters always live close to their mothers.

I worried the essay would be too personal, worried that I had exposed too much, made myself look bad. But I received so many e-mails from readers in response to the column. It taught me that to reach people, you need to dive deep.

"Exposing yourself means writing close to the bone," says Jo-Ann Mapson, author of many novels, including *Goodbye, Earl* and *Blue Rodeo.* "It seems to me that writers are born with one less layer of skin, so that they are privy to hard truths and pain that others might not feel. One has a choice — do I write close to the bone and risk exposure and embarrassment, or do I cloak my stories by using a certain genre or omniscient approach? Or writing about things that are far from my life? All those approaches work, and produce stories, but I favor the close-to-the-bone approach. Readers have asked me what it was like being a twin, how big is my ranch, did I lose a child, and was I ever in a wheelchair. It's a compliment, really, and indicates the story felt authentic even if I haven't experienced all that."

Mystery author Barbara Seranella says her first three books, all unpublished, were about getting divorced. "Now, that's a really unique experience," she says, shaking her head in a self-deprecatory way. "Then a neighbor who was taking a screenwriting class told me the instructor said, 'If you're looking for a plot, take a blank sheet of paper and write down events that have changed your life.' It took me writing those three books about getting divorced to come up with the idea that maybe getting off heroin, being a biker chick and getting out of it, and being an auto mechanic was a world I could take readers to that they wouldn't know otherwise."

And she did. Her first novel, *No Human Involved*, became a national bestseller. She's written more novels with the same main character, Munch Mancini. Seranella gave Munch her own past and pours what she lived through into Munch's character. The result is emotionally gripping crime fiction.

You can't undo what's been done to you, but you can make some sense of it through writing. Use those experiences and create art. There is power in the darkest parts of our lives. It's often apparent in my classes when students put the painful parts on the page. Their voice emerges and their writing comes alive.

"I truly think that writers need to make a list of 'forbidden topics,'" says Mapson, "and then make themselves write about them. Such writing doesn't have to be shared, but it will help to access strong emotions, and strong emotions lead to intense writing. Intense writing can teach a writer how to approach and explore any kind of topic. But if all that stuff is moldering away in the heart, well, it's a kind of constipation that keeps a writer from creating believable, involving stories."

Those dark parts hold power over us. They give us bad dreams at night and they influence our behavior with people in the light of day. When you write about those parts, you help to transfer that invisible but oh-so-tangible power they have over you onto the printed page.

set your timer

If you allowed yourself to, what would be the most difficult things you would write about? What memory keeps leaking through that will not be suppressed? What have you lived through that changed your life? What has happened to you that hasn't happened to anyone else? Begin with who you are right now. As psychotherapist and author Dennis Palumbo says, "You are enough."

Make a list of these events, and be very specific. "The lowest point of my life" or "Things I've done that were embarrassing" or "Things I regret" or "Things that changed my life." So often we quell the urge to reveal ourselves, thinking what we have to say would be boring or might make us look bad. For the moment, look over the list you've made without worrying about what others will think and without running away from what you feel. Accept what you've listed without judging it. Choose one event to write about.

Then, set the timer for fifteen minutes and begin to write. Begin with an action: "When I told him I was leaving, he...," "She came to me, her face long, and she told me...," or any other line that begins in the middle of things.

If you're really stuck, pull out something about yourself that's difficult to expose and disguise it by giving it to a character. Allow all the sorrow, sadness, and tears of this scene, and any other, to clot the page. Don't try to figure out what this is — a story? An essay? The beginning of a novel? Right now, don't burden yourself with those concerns. Just begin writing.

Don't be afraid of what comes out. In all manner of healing, you must first clean the wound and allow the skin to knit until all that's left is a fading scar.

celebrate your otherness

Writers often feel as if they exist on the periphery of life. By being observers, we feel a bit detached from the action of the moment. It's difficult to blend in, to become a part of things. My student Debra Cross says she wishes she could just turn it off, live life like normal folks, but her facility for watching, noting, always makes her feel somehow removed from others.

Another student, Jess Beauchaine, says as long as she can remember, she has always felt like an "other."

"One reason I write is I am a watcher," says Jess. "I love observing my world and trying to make sense of it. It took me so long to come to writing and yet I know beyond a shadow of a doubt that this was what I was made to do, and it is the thing that, rather than making me the same as everyone else (which I don't want to be, I like being 'other,' in some ways), and rather than wishing I were terse, bold, and modern, helps me to embrace my otherness. Writing helps me embrace my life."

My own early life was full of physical rather than intellectual experiences, chosen for me. From four to eight years old, I twirled baton. I didn't love it; my mother wanted me to do it. Twirling segued into modeling. In the dead of winter, in Altoona, Pennsylvania, I modeled a peach and white dress, white Mary Janes, and a white purse on a runway heated by lamps—a co-op venture between Gables department store and the electric company that was promoting new heat-producing lights. During the rehearsals, I studied another boy and girl as they pranced up and down the pseudorunway. How was it that they appeared to be enjoying themselves while I was miserable? The words formed in my mind, directed to my parents: *What about my brain? Can't you love me for that?*

The words never made it out of my mouth, but that was the last time I modeled. I stopped twirling. I buried myself in books, wrote in my diary. Finally, at college, when I started photographing and writing, I began to glimpse who I was, my true self. Which is when I came to understand why I had felt strange so much of my life. I learned to celebrate it. Feeling "other," the awareness and sensitivity that come from both belonging and not belonging, is a source of creativity. Without that awareness, would we be writers?

Dennis Palumbo, author of *Writing from the Inside Out*, and a Los Angeles therapist to writers and other creative types, says, "There's a term in the social sciences called 'participant/observer,' and I think this sums up most writers. I have so many writer patients who describe being at pivotal events in their lives—marriage, birth of a child, a parent's death, etc.—wherein they have all the expected emotions, yet at the same time are 'witnessing' the event as if it were a scene from a novel or film. Some even imagine how they'll recall the event later as though it *were* a scene. A few reveal that, even while experiencing the event in the moment, they're imagining how they'll write the scene later."

Newer writers feel that once they become successful, or established, this otherness will go away. But when I hear accomplished writers discuss otherness, I know it never leaves.

When Alice McDermott came on my show, I asked her if she ever felt more of an observer than participant in life. "If you were totally of the world you probably wouldn't feel compelled to create your own or to remake it in fiction so it's more to your liking. And because my sympathies and identification are more with readers than writers, I depend on fiction writers to pay attention to the things that I can't pay attention to when I'm in the world. That's the thing I hope to offer to my readers: I think that fiction is a kind of meditation that's not singular, it's shared. So if I can offer my readers—busy people doing more important and valuable and concrete things in the world like driving buses and curing diseases—through the written word, the fruits of a certain meditation, then we've paid each other back. So it's not so much that writers need to be out of the world but that they *take* themselves out of the world so that they can give it back to us in a new way."

After that particular show, one of my listeners, Nicholas R. Battista, who has written a novel, e-mailed me straightaway. "When you asked Alice McDermott about writers being outside the world," says Battista, "my ears turned like a dog's toward the speakers. Writers...we are misfits. We're always daydreaming and mentally living in a parallel world to the one in which we physically exist. Even when she talked about her narrator as if he/she were a third person, it struck a chord. Sometimes when I'm writing, I feel detached from it. It's as if I were a witness to my own imagination. It's as if I'm not a participant in it at all. At the end of the session, it's almost like someone else did the writing."

This feeling of otherness manifests itself in all sorts of ways, and often with our families.

"I'm driving in the car with the kids and it's not that I'm not paying attention to the road," says author Susan Straight, "but if they are quiet, talking among themselves, I'm thinking of my characters and what they're doing, or I'll hear a song and I'm in that fictional world. Toni Morrison gave an interview once where she talked about this, and she said it's almost like there's a scrim of water between her and her children—not in a bad way, but that's just the way our brains work when we're writers, so I felt better after I read that. It's not that I'm not paying complete attention when we're studying the tundra and rainforest."

Thank goodness we writers discovered who we were when we did. Imagine all the poor souls who traverse life never knowing, who try to draw enjoyment from interactions that will never sustain them. It seems a form of grace to learn who you are early enough (Read: At least before you are on your deathbed and your life flashes before your eyes) to do something with it. We have that opportunity as creative beings to do something with our otherness.

 set your timer

Remember when you first felt like the other. Who were you with and what were you doing? Paint the experience with words. Was there a moment when you realized the reason you felt like the other was because your innate concerns, your frame of reference, were different? Where was this? What changed? Was it a life-altering event? Did your life look and feel a bit different afterward? Often this happens for new writers in the midst of a class. They remember the absolute moment they realized they were different and they remember what they were doing — usually writing.

One way to stave off the feeling of being a misfit is to join a writers group or make friends with at least one other writer whom you can talk to and share ideas and feelings about writing. In the chapter "Keep Your Lips Sealed," Dennis Palumbo talks about how having just one writing buddy can seem like a miracle.

Set the timer and write for fifteen minutes about how it felt to be an other and what you feel like now, now that you've identified yourself as a writer, are beginning to know other writers, and are on the path.

> *The one thing all nations of the*
> *earth share is the fear that a member of*
> *the family will want to be an artist.*
> —Robert Frost

using the ones you love

Multiple marriages, remarriages, and bigamy run in my family. My dad married my mother while he was still married to his first wife. My half sister divorced her first husband, married her second husband, divorced him, and remarried the first; and when he died, she remarried the second, who had been waiting for her for ten years. My half brother divorced then remarried his wife. My blood brother has been married and divorced three times. My mother married twice. I'm on my third marriage. (Three's a charm...)

Sound confusing to you? How do you think I feel? Still, it's all material, every last convoluted morsel. Flannery O'Connor said if you make it through childhood, you have enough stories to last a lifetime. My repository of family material to write about could take me into my golden years, I'm sure.

My mother has found her way into poems, short stories, essays, and a novel—some published, some not. While I've been careful not to publish anything deliberately hurtful to her while she was alive, now after her death, I'm not sure she would always like the ways I've portrayed her. Yet, if we are true to ourselves, and we follow the words that need to be written, we have little control over what we write. Our subject matter chooses us. When we listen, when we pay attention, we follow the cue and some of our best writing results.

Of course we can deny that which wants to be written and write what is easy and nice and causes no inner churnings. Yet, most of us begin here. "Everyone has trauma, even if your family is normal," says my friend, the author Allison Johnson. "Where else are you going to start?"

Diane Leslie's novels, *Fleur de Leigh's Life of Crime* and *Fleur de Leigh in Exile*, are loosely based on her upbringing in Hollywood. Leslie grew up with nannies—about sixty of them in all—and so made the character of the mother quite colorful, but not the sort of mom you'd want for your own.

Yet, Leslie's mother not only attends her book signings, she also signs her daughter's books. She's delighted to be immortalized in print. Leslie showed her mother the manuscript for her first novel before she submitted it to her publisher to make sure her mother would not take offense. Her mother loved it.

"I gave the manuscript to my mother and said, 'If you find anything objectionable, I'll take it out.' I didn't want to make her miserable. I have no bigger fan than my mother. I continue to write about her. There's more and more."

When authors fear hurting someone, they may wait until that person has died. When Frances Mayes, author of *Under the Tuscan Sun*, came on my show, I asked her about using questionable family material. "Lots of writers struggle with that," she says. "My friend Molly Giles was asked by a student, 'How can you write about your parents like this?' And she said, 'That's what God gave them to you for.' I think that would be a freeing attitude, but I feel protective toward my family; if they don't want things written about them, then I don't want to write about them. It's just an ethical question people answer in various ways and I can understand either way."

Writers hailing from cultures where there is a strong ethic of silence, of not sharing stories of how it is to be the underdog, may worry more about how their work will affect family members. Italians, I've found from personal experience, have such a culture. We may overcome our fear, but it never leaves us entirely.

I asked Maria Laurino, author of *Were You Always an Italian?* if she worried about her family reading her book. "I was very worried," says Laurino. "I thought about it constantly. At one point when the copyedited manuscript was going to be published, I thought, Maybe I'll just store it under the bed somewhere and it'll reappear five years from now. Yet, I felt the issues I was writing about were so important to me and I tried to deal with them as honestly and truthfully as I could. So I went ahead and I'm glad I did. I think the book overall has been a very positive experience."

Mary Yukari Waters, author of a short story collection, *The Laws of Evening*, says, "One advantage I have is that no one in my family in Japan reads or speaks English, and that's great. I don't know if I could do this if they were American and lived right here. It's a big dilemma. I'm not the kind of person who feels you can use anything for the sake of art."

It's a balancing act: how much to reveal, how much to keep off the page, and what self-exposure will result in. A student, Candice Harper, who recently won a PEN Emerging Authors Award, says, "I'm really apprehensive about the day I publish my novel and my grandmother (who's my heroine), my grandfather (the pastor I don't want to embarrass), or my daughters (whose respect means so much to me) actually read it and analyze what it says about me. I'm afraid people I care about will think it's autobiographical where it isn't and overlook the parts of me that are actually there on the page. I worry about these things—but not when I'm writing. Those are thoughts that contribute to writer's block. If I worry that my husband or parents or daughters will judge me based on what my fictional characters say and do, I stumble. It's like thinking about whether or not the workshop will respond to my piece. Those kinds of thoughts make me try too hard and the result is forced and stilted. This rarely happens to me, because I stifle myself in so many other parts of my life, that the page becomes the one space where most of it finds a place."

You may share these fears. Most of us do. But if you allow these fears to stop you, you'll never write. Your words will remain closed up inside you, growing moldy like your least favorite shoes at the back of your closet.

Author Amy Bloom says, "I write, as much as possible, with my eyes closed (literally, for sex scenes) and certainly with my mind's eye closed to the world. When I write, I have no parents, no children, no spouse to be shocked or distressed. There are things about my kids' lives I don't use, because I think they would feel violated, and there are other things from my past that I keep the lid on, but in my imagination, it is my universe only and there are no observers."

Truth is, your family will probably never even read your work unless you put it in front of their noses, and even then they may not. And if they do, you may be surprised at their reactions. Jo-Ann Mapson says that over time her family isn't bothered by what she writes, though "they see me as quirky or strange because of who I am and what I do, and my mother does think I swear too much."

Certainly, some families do not approve of what their family member turned author has written, and what then? Authors have alienated their parents or siblings because of what they've revealed. But more often than not, this is just not the case. When you write fiction, you obviously embellish, fictionalize. And even when you've closely based a character on, say, your mother, inevitably she won't recognize herself.

But when you're in the midst of writing, don't worry about the future. When you write, make sure everyone you know isn't looking over your shoulder. Don't think about your friends, your relatives, and especially your parents. You don't want to end up writing only what's pleasant and acceptable.

Writing about your family members is one way of working out the more difficult aspects of your relationships with them, which you may never get the chance to do in real life. In the last years of her life, so much went unsaid between my mother and me. When she died two years ago after suffering from Alzheimer's, I could pretty much forget about closure. So now I do the next best thing; I do what writers do. I occasionally write about her. It helps me sort it out.

Yes, it's difficult writing about your parents and those close to you. Yes, it's heart wrenching. But if you don't put down on paper all of these different emotions, they will eat away at you.

Your parents gave you more than life—they gave you a great wealth of material to take you through your writing days. Use this legacy and be grateful for it.

➶ set your timer

No one has your family or your upbringing. If you were to tell someone about five things that you feel are different about your family, what would you tell them? What were (are) your family's rituals? Is your father or mother a character unto him- or herself? What was your upbringing like?

Look through photo albums, letters, and family scrapbooks. What catches your eye? Study photographs and see if you can remember other details of the day certain pictures were taken. What was that day about? Where were you? What sort of things did the people in the photo say? What were their concerns then?

You might also make a list headed "My family" and write down everything you remember about them. You could cluster these details: In the center of a sheet of paper draw a circle that says "My family." Then start drawing lines from that circle to other smaller circles. In them write "Mother," "Father," "Aunt Teresa" and so on. From those circles, draw smaller circles. Attached to Aunt Teresa's circle might be a circle that says, "owned a boutique," "traveled to Venice," "took the train to work." Get as many relatives as you can think of onto this sheet of paper and detail each.

Make a list of the high points, weird points, surprises in your life. Who is your most interesting relative? What makes him or her interesting? What about family tragedies or mistakes, or even regrets?

You might also ponder what you have always wanted to write but worry about who might see it and be offended. If you haven't already, right now make a list of those events or moments, and be as specific as possible: "When I caught Mom hugging Mr. Barefoot." "That time I was in the car with Jim Lane and he got pulled over on Church Street and arrested for methamphetamine." "When I was in seventh grade and sat on a log in the woods behind our Elbow Lane house smoking with June Leach."

Once you have a list of twelve or so items, pick one. You may feel terrified to even put these things down on paper. You never need show a soul, but you must give yourself permission to voice your experiences and write what you believe is the unwriteable. Now, set the timer for fifteen minutes and see where your words take you.

I can remember the lush spring excitement
of language in childhood. Sitting in church, rolling it
around in my mouth like marbles—tabernacle and Pharisee
and parable, trespasses and Babylon and covenant.
—Penelope Lively, MOON TIGER

breaking the chains

Finding your way to the writing life is a serpentine path, at best. Look at writers' childhoods and it's hard to see how the years led up to their becoming a writer.

There were no writers in my family, not even readers of books. We didn't have conversations around the dinner table, at least not in English. My father came from Sicily when he was a teen and my mother was a first-generation Italian American. My parents often spoke Italian around the house. It was their secret language. Early on I stopped trying to understand what they were saying. I retreated to my room and read or wrote in my diary or made up stories for my paper dolls.

My mother, with her seventh-grade education and parents who never learned English, had a weak grasp of the language. Her speech was a sauce made up of Italian and English. She called ricotta "legote." *Pasta e fagiole* was "vassavasul." Around our dinner table, if you wanted someone to pass the crusty Italian bread, you said,

"Gimme the bread," not "Will you please pass the bread?" "Lie" was "lay," "gone" was "went," and "I get you" meant "I understand."

In retrospect, the lack of language in our home was one reason that, as a child, I went to church. While my mother and brother slept in, Dad dropped me off at St. Mark's and proceeded on to the drugstore down the street for a cup of coffee, a cigarette, and the Sunday paper. At Mass among the stained glass windows and song, I absorbed music and language. I didn't understand the Latin mass, but I loved hearing it spoken.

When I went to college many years later, writing was the most difficult thing I had ever tried to do. My vocabulary was teensy, I mangled grammar: How would I ever write? Photography, the visual arts, and performing arts came easy, but expressing thoughts and feelings in words presented a seemingly insurmountable challenge. I had little access to the words to describe exactly what I was going through or what something looked like or smelled like. The most challenging thing I could do with my life was learn to write, even though why I was compelled to remains a mystery still.

It's encouraging to know that many accomplished writers also came from nonliterary backgrounds. Award-winning poet Stephen Dunn told me, "I literally grew up in a house without books and no one ever went to college."

Novelist Susan Straight says, "I came from a completely nonacademic background. Many of my friends now still are illiterate. I hang out most of the time with people who don't read at all; a lot of them can't. When I got to graduate school, I still said things like, 'We shouldn't have went over there,' and people would look at me with expressions that said, What are you talking about? People in workshop at graduate school would also say to me, 'So, what's with all the working-class background?' I didn't even know what working class was. I went home and looked up working class. I had no idea that it was a bad thing; I didn't know there was a leisure class. In my neighborhood, if you had a job, that was a good thing. If you weren't working class, you were homeless."

While it may seem that there are more weaknesses than strengths in being from a nonwriting family, you make up for it by bringing to your writing a knowledge of the street and the firsthand experience of life as it is lived by the majority of people.

set your timer

Who were you when you were a child? Take out your notebook, or sit at your computer, and drift back. Set your timer for fifteen minutes. What did your parents want you to be? Who did they think you were? Did it jibe with how you saw yourself?

What were family dinners like? What did you talk about? Did you vacation as a family? Write about one that stands out.

Is there a particular moment that resonates with the knowledge that you weren't the person your parents wanted you to be, that you could never, in fact, be that person, and that you were a writer? Or did you find yourself in a career that was all wrong?

What made you think you were a writer? Write about this, and let yourself feel it, with all its attendant emotion.

Familiarity. Memory of the way things
get said. Once you have heard certain expressions,
sentences, you almost never forget them.
—Eudora Welty

words can be so powerful

Words are so powerful they can resonate in our minds and hearts forever. The words someone said to you when you were a child that filled you with pain or joy, or a story someone told you that affected you in a certain way, can have a lasting effect.

Would you marry me anyway, even if there wasn't a pink dot? A pregnancy test sat on the bathroom counter. I followed the directions on the box and waited ten minutes. When the dot turned pink, I was stunned. Even Leao, our Portuguese water dog, looked befuddled. Brian and I had been living together for almost six months. He had said he hoped there was a pink dot. I wasn't sure I believed him. Many years back, while in college, I got pregnant. The painter I lived with had not responded positively—at all. "What do you want to do about it?" was about all he said. That said it all. I will never forget the tone of his voice, his lifeless green eyes.

When Brian walked through the door, I stood by the sofa, holding up the white plastic stick like a thermometer, watching his eyes.

He saw the look on my face and said, "It was pink." I said, "Yes," and held it out to him so he could see the dot. The sweetest smile bloomed on his face. As he knelt, he pulled a black velvet box from his pocket, opened it, and removed an opal ring.

"Will you marry me?" he said.

"Yes," I said, "I'll marry you."

"Would you anyway, even if there wasn't a pink dot?"

All of life is material when you're a writer. Words can change the direction of your life. What the painter said to me, and my husband's words later, mark turning points in my life.

The incident with the painter more than twenty years ago, the more recent scene with my husband, and the words both men said, have stayed with me. The painter's words were so powerful that they became the genesis for a long short story ("Quickening") that I wrote and eventually published in the *Oyez Review* and a second short story I started several months ago. Brian's words launched a magazine column on good fathers and became the inspiration for a character in a novel in progress. I imagine that the words each man uttered packed enough wallop to fuel my writing for some time to come.

The stories people tell you can be a powerful stimulus for your writing, even if what they say has nothing to do with you and everything to do with them. T. Jefferson Parker, author of *Cold Pursuit*, was recently a guest on my radio show and talked about how such a story inspired that book.

"Years ago my little brother Matt told me about something that happened when he went away to sea right after high school—I'm guessing it was 1974, 1975," says Parker. "For four to five months he worked at sea on a commercial tuna boat. When they returned, he was told the money he earned would pay for his food and supplies on the boat and that he would get paid nothing. It stuck in my craw, his story, a young man being taken advantage of, and a tale like his forms the kernel of the story that takes place in *Cold Pursuit*."

set your timer

Can you remember words someone said to you that changed the direction of your life? Hearing or saying the words "I do" or "I'm having an affair" can send your life veering into new, unexpected realms.

Has someone told you a story that, as Parker said, stuck in your craw? What was said? Take fifteen minutes and write down your memories.

Why shouldn't truth be stranger than
fiction? Fiction, after all, has to make sense.
— Mark Twain

life imitating art

S ome time ago I worked on a novel in which the main character drove a Cadillac. Not just any Cadillac, but a big old white
Cadillac as long as my living room is wide. When I gave that character a Caddy, I myself had no desire for a Caddy, nor plans to ever
buy one. My father drove Cadillacs most of his life, but I have always
been an import sort of gal.

But fate had other plans; it often does. A few years ago, two weeks
before Christmas, my Toyota got totaled by a drunk driver and I
needed a car—immediately. Being a freelance writer, I preferred
one without car payments. I also craved lots of padding and metal,
the kind of car that I could get hit in and not realize it for at least a
week.

I began silently chanting, *Big car, big car, big car.* And then this
'78 Caddy landed in my life.

Talk about life imitating art. How *does* it happen? I find it's more
common than I thought.

On my radio show, novelist Jacquelyn Mitchard talked about how life has often mirrored her books. "When I was writing *The Most Wanted*, I was a widow and dated every orthodontist in southern Wisconsin. I said, 'There's no one that thinks a woman in her early forties with four children under the age of twelve is a dream date.' So I made up, in my book, the husband I would want. I met him the day the book was printed, *the day it arrived*, and how eerily like my character Charlie Wilder he was. It astonished us both. My agent says I should make up a book about a woman and her agent who win the Irish sweepstakes!"

Who knows how and why it happens, but when life imitates art, it is life-affirming. It's as if the universe is saying, you are on the right page, your art and your life are in sync. It's God's way of saying, "Go for it!"

set your timer

Write about an example of wishes coming true in your life that no one would believe if it were in a short story or a novel. Or write about something that happened that was just too strange, that you yourself would have a hard time believing, if it hadn't happened to you.

Perhaps you dreamed something that later came true or maybe it was your day off and you found yourself thinking of someone you work with and then ran into that person. Take that real-life occurrence and begin with it, then embellish, exaggerate, and go wild.

A hobby a day keeps the doldrums away.
—Phyllis McGinley, A Pocketful of Wry

beads of sweat ... or pleasure

I must confess. I'm obsessed. And it's not just with writing: I also have a minor craving for work so different that for months I was quite closemouthed about it.

It's beading. I love to bead. I love beads of all kinds—vintage, pearls, semiprecious gemstones. The interesting thing is, this hobby came to me by way of my writing.

Two years ago I wrote a story for the *Los Angeles Times Magazine* about Mimi Anzaldo, a beader friend of mine. When I visited Mimi in her studio on the other side of town, she had just returned from a major bead show in Tucson, Arizona, with more than $5,000 worth of beads. Beads in an array of candy colors filled bags, lay on the table on strings, stuffed her trays and plastic boxes.

As we began talking, I felt the obsession for beads take hold once again. In college, I made beaded jewelry and sold it at the cafeteria during lunch. This was one way I put myself through school as I studied to become a writer. When I got my degree, I put my beads away, but kept them with me in plastic bags on moves from Vermont to San Francisco to Southern California.

After seeing Mimi, I went home and got out my bags of beads. In the coming weeks, I started visiting bead stores and bead shows, and shopped for beads online. At times it was difficult remembering writing was my priority. I made my deadlines, but I beaded when I thought I should have been writing and felt guilty. I stayed up late into the night. I had spent a few hundred dollars and had made a couple of dozen necklaces and earrings—more than I'd ever wear—when Cheryl Pruett, a writer friend, came to see what I'd been up to. My good friend was prepared to buy one trinket, just to show her support. But she ended up trying everything on and spending $150. Without intending to, I had started a part-time business. I had to; if I wanted to keep beading, I had to sell what I made.

Other than a few close friends, I told no contacts in the writing world about my hobby. I worried they would take me less seriously as a writer if they knew I was also obsessed with something other than writing. Finally, I "came out" in my biweekly column. I wrote:

> Last week when my friend, fellow writer, and former student Allison Johnson came over and bought a pair of earrings and a bracelet, she said, "You really have a gift for this beading thing. Are you giving up writing?" It struck me: the belief still exists, however subconsciously, that you can't do more than one thing at a time. While I don't believe this, I've learned many women are dealing with this false dilemma.

I had never considered giving up writing for beading. Each fulfilled such a different part of me. Still, I did feel guilty and wondered why. Perhaps it's because it's already so hard, as a woman, being taken seriously as a writer, and doing a craft just adds a sense of amateurism. Roberta Wax, a freelance writer, college writing instructor, and former United Press International reporter, creates jewelry and cards. She says it's because she fears losing credibility that she doesn't tell her journalist friends about her secret life as an artisan.

But I believe that beading is good for my writing because it provides such a complementary creative outlet. Writing is all about words, thoughts, ideas, feelings. Beading is about color, texture, and quiet. I space out when I'm beading and allow whatever writing I'm working on to simmer at a subconscious level. Then, when I return to writing, I feel refreshed.

And, actually, if your craft or other hobby gets to the point where it can generate money, it can take the pressure off your writing. Since I started selling my beaded beauties, I have become pickier about which writing jobs and assignments I take on; I can often make as much or more with jewelry than on certain assignments, and that allows me to turn down jobs that don't thrill me.

Another writer friend, Karen Berger, recently added teaching piano to her schedule. "I found myself frustrated with the increasingly unfair contracts that are often being forced on writers today," says Berger, the author of nine books, including her most recent, *More Everyday Wisdom: Trail-Tested Advice from the Experts.* "Teaching piano gave me, after thirteen years of solitary freelance writing, a chance to meet people in the community and interact with them. It exercises different creative muscles in my brain, it's a lot of fun, and it gives me a regular cash flow while still allowing me to set my own hours. And it gives me the ability to pursue and take on interesting writing projects and to decline projects that don't pay well, aren't interesting, or require me to sign contracts that I find abusive. The result has been beneficial for me in every way—financially, creatively, socially, and in terms of my feelings of independence and security."

Hobbies can also serve as inspirations for articles and essays, or can become the avocations, or professions, of your fictional characters. Judith Ryan Hendricks's love of baking segued into writing two food-related novels, *Bread Alone* and *Isabel's Daughters.* T. Jefferson Parker's hobby of keeping snakes served as inspiration for one of his novels, *Where Serpents Lie.* Earlene Fowler's quilt collecting became the motif of her long-running mystery series. Ann Packer's love of sewing found its way into her bestselling novel, *The Dive from Clausen's Pier.*

Writing about hobbies is also a natural spark for essays and articles. Los Angeles–based freelance writer and longtime scrapbooker Kathy Sena wrote an essay for *Woman's Day* about creating a scrapbook with her son. The idea arose from her feeling disheartened to see her friends stress over wanting to create scrapbooks for their kids.

"They knew their pages could never look like the fancy pages in scrapbooking magazines," says Sena. "My point was that it's the memories—the handprints, the journaling about funny little things that happen, the fun stuff of family life—and not the fancy doodads that matter."

Or your hobby may be for pure enjoyment. Former U.S. poet laureate Billy Collins says, "I like to draw as a relief. I've been drawing ever since I was in graduate school because I realized as I was studying for my qualifying examinations I was losing my mind to a completely verbal universe, so I bought some expensive drawing pens and started doing contour drawings as a way to reconnect myself to the visual. Ever since then, I like to draw."

Writers so easily become guilty over one thing or another. Don't feel guilty for having a hobby you don't want to replace with writing. Give yourself permission to take seriously whatever helps you live life your way. Keep the hobby, and keep writing. Both are good.

set your timer

Take fifteen minutes and write a sketch of a character who engages in your hobby or obsession—a silversmith, boatbuilder, beekeeper, orchid grower, pastry chef, race car driver. See where it takes you. You may find that fifteen minutes is not enough, that you want to continue with the character and turn the piece into a story. Channel your own experiences and passion into a believable character, and establish a balance between self-exposure and fiction.

By knowing this hobby or avocation as you do, you will bring a certain honesty and verisimilitude to the character, and to your story. As Ayelet Waldman and Michael Chabon have said, everyone thinks it's about you anyway, so have fun with it.

Or write an essay about this passion of yours. Take the reader into your world. What is this hobby of yours and why does it engage you so? Give us the details. Show us how it fuels your fervor and why.

craft

Contrary to what many of you might imagine, a career in letters is not without its drawbacks—chief among them the unpleasant fact that one is frequently called upon to actually sit down and write.
—Fran Lebowitz, METROPOLITAN LIFE

form

The chapters in this section should give you a taste of the various elements that go into good writing, but they aren't intended to be the final word on the subject of craft. The exercises that close these chapters will get you on the right track, and the many good books listed in the bibliography will keep you there and take you further.

By now you know how to get started writing, how to find inspiration when you need it, and how to overcome writing obstacles. Now consider what it is that you are creating.

Before you build anything, you need to know *what* you're building. Form is the foundation upon which you assemble the content of your writing. Imagine building a house without a foundation and without knowing what the finished structure is going to look like. Will it be a stucco house or a brownstone, a craftsman cottage, condo, postmodern construction, or yurt?

The architecture, the *scope*, of your idea determines what the context, structure, and form should be. Who are your ideal readers and how can you reach them? Do you want to spend a couple of weeks with your idea or a couple of years? What do you want this piece of writing to do—explain, persuade, entertain, evoke a feeling, make someone pick up the phone or a picket sign? For instance, are you interested in expressing an opinion about the construction going on at your child's school? Sounds like an opinion piece for the op-ed page of your local newspaper. Are you moved to write about your mother, or about being a mother? Could be a Mother's Day essay for a women's magazine. Do you want to write about two high school sweethearts who meet again at a reunion and decide to take up where they left off twenty years ago? Could be a short story, unless the story is of epic proportions and you're confident you'll be interested in it for the next year or two, in which case it might be a novel. Or it, too, could be an article or an essay. It depends.

"When I write an essay, it has to be something I feel passionate about," says Susan Straight. "I wrote a piece for the *Los Angeles Times Magazine* called 'Bubble Wrapping Baby' that started because all the playgrounds at school were being wrapped with yellow tape and I felt sad that our kids can't do some of the things we did. I felt passionate about it in a completely different way from how I feel about a novel. I wrote a short story about a female correctional officer and her nephew at the prison where she works that was in *Zoetrope*. It came from feeling sad to see a lot of my nieces and nephews being incarcerated and not knowing what to do about it. That's when I write fiction; when something is scary to me or very sad, it's something I don't think I can fix. When I write an essay, I'm getting feelings out on paper or I'll be reading it on NPR [and] I have what is probably a misguided notion that someone will relate to it. Fiction is so much more private and scary."

You don't always know exactly what you're writing until you begin and work your way into the piece. You may begin writing about cream cheese, sure you have enough to fill a book, but after five hundred words you've said all you have to say about cream cheese. On the other hand, you might begin writing about heart disease in women and find that an article-length piece is not nearly enough room to explore and say all you are moved to say. Or you may have an intense nugget of feeling or a powerful image that can be nothing other than a poem.

"For me, poems cannot be expressed any other way," says Lynne Sharon Schwartz, who is known for her novels. "Poems can't be reduced to straight realism the way a realistic novel can. A story and an essay are harder to distinguish. I started my novel, *Leaving Brooklyn*, as an essay, but I had an urge to make things up. What I wanted to do was not inform the reader, but to make a structure, like a piece of sculpture, that the reader would walk around and see whatever he or she could see. With an essay, there's more of a desire to give information. With fiction, you want to make a shape, put a new object into the world. It's a matter of instinct. You have to divine: What do you want to do with this thing? Sometimes it comes with a label; it announces: I am a story, I am an essay, I am a poem. It's the ones that come without their labels, such as *Leaving Brooklyn*, that you may have to fuss around with and do in the wrong form for a while until you realize the true label."

That's what happened with Judith Ryan Hendricks, author of *Bread Alone*. She took a UCI Extension creative nonfiction class and her first assignment was to write an essay about something she loved to do and why. She wrote about making bread.

"The essay morphed into more than an essay and I started embroidering a little bit," she says. "I wasn't really telling the truth so it couldn't be considered nonfiction, creative or otherwise. It eventually took possession of me and became a novel. I always thought it would be great to write a novel but never thought I could sustain an effort over that long period of time, and it *was* long—it took me four years to write *Bread Alone.*"

Over and over I hear mystery writers talk about how the structure of a mystery helped them to write their book and finish it. "I never read many mysteries and I still don't," says Elizabeth George, "but when I was a teacher I taught a class about the mystery and after three years, I began to think I could write one myself. It provided a structure on which I could hang anything I wanted to hang, and I knew by the end of the book I'd have to solve the crime."

set your timer

Take an idea, the *content*, and try on different *contexts*, or structures. Try the same idea in various forms. Write it as a poem, an essay, a short story. Which form seems to best capture what you're trying to do? What changes when you use the same idea for an essay and a story? Which better helps you to express that idea? Which is the most fun?

As you pore over newspapers, magazines, and literary journals, stop and ponder whether what you're reading might be more interesting if it took on a different form, or, at the very least, how it would change.

Take a stab at it. Choose a piece—better a short piece than long—and read it a few times. Then put it aside, and using it as a prompt, write for fifteen minutes. Where does it take you? You may discover something you wanted to say that you had no idea was in you. The act of discovery, unearthing what it is we're thinking and feeling passionate about, is one of writing's greatest joys.

plot or not

Outlining and plotting...necessary evils? There are no absolutes when it comes to writing a story, article, essay, or novel. Some writers say you must know your entire story, outline it, and plot it out before you write it; other writers feel if they know everything before they start, it will take away all the fun.

Most of my students who are working on novels have such a hard time with plot. It's the narrative drive of your work, I tell them, but that sounds so abstract. Narrative drive? What the heck is narrative drive? I circle back to the reader: It's what makes the reader turn the page. It's what makes the reader stay up past her bedtime so she can read one more chapter. When there's no narrative drive, the work is lackluster. The writing can be to die for, but the story is so static it makes you fall asleep.

Another way to think of plot is, what does your main character want, what is her purpose, and what obstacles can you put in her way? What is the *trouble*? Trouble, obstacles, challenges...these will create tension and conflict and will drive your character to succeed, or fail.

A mystery or thriller tends to be more plot-driven than, say, a literary novel. While some mystery authors will say they don't know the exact ending of their book or each plot point when they start writing, by the time they stop, they have to make sure the pieces of their story all fit together.

Crime writer Laura Lippman says, "If you're willing to do a lot of drafts—and I am—you can back your way into a pretty well-constructed plot. A lot of people are terrified of rewrites. My journalism background is so helpful in terms of being freed from the fear of having to start completely over again. If you've worked at a newspaper, chances are you've done a medium-to-lengthy feature that you've turned in and have had turned back to you and it's almost like a fish that has been deboned. You essentially have to do it over. You've got the lead in the middle and the middle is the end and the end is—you've got to rethink it. But once you've done that a couple of times, you realize it's survivable. Plots are not that hard to fix if you're willing to work them over and over again. I like going through draft after draft after draft. By the time I'm on my fourth draft of something, I've got a really good grasp of the story that I started with and I know everything about it, but it's not until that fourth draft."

Bestselling crime writer T. Jefferson Parker tends to outline. "I outline the broader concerns as well as I can. If you can solve the big riddles of story before you begin writing, you're ahead of the game, although I've written entire novels based on no outline at all, which is an exciting, sometimes perilous, way to make a story."

Mystery writer Elizabeth George says she visits potential settings with a kernel of a plot—the killer, the victim, the motive—and sometimes she doesn't even have that much. "Sometimes I only have a scene," she says. "Like the idea of the body of a schoolboy being found at the side of a road in England. That was the idea for *Well-Schooled in Murder*. But I didn't know who killed him or why. Visiting the locations made it apparent to me. It was by going to England and seeing the place that I was able to come up with the story. If I was doing it at home in California, everything would be very generic. I'm not good at cooking up a location since my plots are dependent on location."

Literary novels are more character-driven and language-focused. They don't require plotting the way mysteries do. Yet the best literary novels have a strong narrative.

Many authors allow plot to emerge from the characters. Put two characters together and see what happens. And something *will* happen, if you let it. Plunk them down in a setting, give them a problem, and watch them go. Some authors begin with the question: "What if?" Jacquelyn Mitchard, author of *The Deep End of the Ocean*, says, "For me the question that all of my stories start with is, 'What if?' What if this circumstance were to happen, how would you handle it, how would you cope, how would you respond? And then I put characters into those situations and see how they try to get themselves out of trouble or find some saving grace in a difficult situation."

Some literary authors simply need a rough outline. When Robert Stone, author of *Bay of Souls*, came on my show, I asked him about plotting. "I make little summaries of the chapters so they fit," he said. "Plot drives me crazy. I'm not a dedicated realist. I really prefer poetry and magic to strict realism. At the same time, I think you owe people a story, so I try to keep the story straight; I don't subject people to things that couldn't have happened."

"I do little plotting," says Chris Bohjalian. "I never had any notion with any of my books how they were going to end when I began them. And speaking selfishly, that certainly made the writing process infinitely more enjoyable for me. Because I don't know where they're going, writing is just massive amounts of fun."

Janet Fitch, author of *White Oleander*, says she didn't plot that novel but wrote it in scenes. After she wrote a scene, she threw it in a box. When her box was full, she took them out of the box, three-hole punched them, and tried to organize them into some sort of a flow, seeing what would never fit anywhere and what remained to be written.

When you base your fiction on a true story or something that actually happened, the plot is a given. Tracy Chevalier says, "With *Girl with a Pearl Earring*, I did know the plot because it's very clear that it's going to end with a painting. She goes to the household in the beginning and you know in the end the painter is going to paint her; it's on the cover of the book so it can't be anything different. I knew the peaks and the arc of the story before I started writing. With *Falling Angels*, I didn't. After I finished the first draft—it was in third person—I completely tore it apart and retold it from twelve characters' points of view."

There are hefty texts, like Janet Burroway's *Writing Fiction*, that explore outline and plot far more than I do here. My intent is to get you thinking and help you to figure out what kind of writer you are. If you want to read more, pick up Burroway's book, or any one of the many books that explore the topic, some of which are listed in the bibliography.

set your timer

I call this one the Chinese menu exercise. This is how you begin: On a sheet of paper create three columns. At the top of one column, write the word "Character." At the top of the second write "Setting," and at the top of the third write "Situation."

In each column write four words on four different lines. Under character you might write, "Waitress," "Pianist," "Soccer champ," and "Dentist." Under setting, you might jot down, "The dog days of summer," "the Lincoln tunnel," "the desert outside Las Vegas," and "a lamp factory." In the third column, under "Situation," you might write, "The police arrive at the door," "Wins the lotto," "Discovers spouse in a compromising position," and "Accidentally hits a boxer dog with car."

Now, pick one from each column, set the timer for fifteen minutes, and begin writing. You have a character, a setting, and a situation—all that you need to create a work of fiction. What dictates the drama of the story? Do the characters or does the situation drive the plot?

While this isn't a freewriting exercise, don't give it too much thought, lest you spend most of your fifteen minutes thinking and not writing.

Tension is created in those
delicious moments of anxious uncertainty.
—Sol Stein

creating tension

The writer's job is to keep the reader turning the page. In fiction and in some narrative nonfiction, as well as having a strong story or plot, tension or suspense is necessary. Doesn't matter whether the fiction you're writing is mainstream or literary, a romance or a mystery. All fiction needs an element of suspense.

Beginning writers often make the mistake of plopping a crisis in a story without adequate buildup. For example, one minute your main character, Naomi, is relaxing on a chaise lounge by the pool, sipping a piña colada. The next moment the water is erupting from the pool because there's been a 6.0 earthquake. The result for the reader is, Ho hum. The scene could have been suspenseful, but the writer did not build up to the pivotal moment.

But what if the writer had Naomi sipping her piña colada as she felt something strange in the air, something she couldn't put her finger on. She hears the distant howl of a dog, then another dog, then the hair on the back of her head stands up as she hears a louder sound, then a rumble as the ground begins to quake. People begin to panic, and a waiter, carrying a tray of drinks on his shoulder, loses his footing and the drinks come crashing down on the cement. Then the water rises from the pool like a geyser.

You get the picture. Build the suspense slowly, from a sense of calm to a fevered pitch, and you'll keep the reader turning the page.

Real-life daily occurrences can teach you about suspense, and how it moves. Here's one from a few years ago that taught me.

The day was mild, sunny. I was out back working in the studio. It was high noon, and I had another half hour before Brian had to go, leaving me to care for Travis. Just as I was thinking about how wonderful it was that I had a few more minutes to write, Brian, who becomes frantic when anything happens that the least bit resembles an emergency bursts into my office and says, "Lindsey's babysitter is locked out of the house. Lindsey's inside. Call a locksmith." Then he disappears, presumably back across the street to tell the babysitter that help is on the way.

My first thought is, Why can't he do it? It's my time to concentrate on my writing. Then it registers: *This is an emergency. Forget about yourself.*

I get out the Yellow Pages and call a locksmith ad that says in big bold letters: EMERGENCY SERVICE. A man picks up on the first ring. "We've got an emergency situation here," I say. He says he'll be here in ten, fifteen minutes.

I run across the street to the back of our neighbor's house, where Brian, Travis, and the babysitter are looking through the kitchen door at baby Lindsey sitting on the wood floor. She stares back at us, still fairly calm. Brian returns home while Travis and I and the babysitter wave at Lindsey, praying she doesn't stray from sight into the bathroom or some other room, or that she doesn't open a kitchen drawer and pull out a knife. I study the glass panes of the window on the door, wondering how hard it would be to break one pane without the glass reaching Lindsey.

Ten minutes later the locksmith still hasn't arrived. Lindsey starts to cry. I pick up Travis, ask him to wave at her. Babies like kids' faces, so this keeps her interested for a spell. But then she begins to cry harder. Finally we hear the screech of wheels on the street in front of the house.

The babysitter rushes around front to get the locksmith. He's wearing black wraparound sunglasses. He clutches a small lock-picking kit. I begin to wonder if it's easy for anyone to get a kit like this and if locksmiths are ever accused of breaking into houses.

He kneels in front of the doorknob and jiggles the lock as the baby's cries accelerate. I chew the inside of my mouth, trying to quell the tears about to pour from my eyes, too. Lindsey comes to the door, holds on to the doorknob. She's hysterical now, trying to turn the knob, while the locksmith is jiggling, cursing under his breath, beginning to sweat. "Talk about pressure," he grumbles.

But then he says, "Yes!" and the lock opens.

Fiction writers create suspense in a variety of ways, but one thing is certain: It's got to build quickly. Mystery novelist Martha C. Lawrence says, "I've been reading literally dozens of books back to back for the Shamus and Edgar Awards, and it's very evident (as it was when I was an editor) that if the author doesn't capture the reader's attention in the first two pages, the book is likely to be put back on the shelf."

Susanna Moore creates tension by building up conflict. "There has to be a problem, and that problem has to take your hero or heroine on a journey in which there is, even in Aristotelian terms, conflict and then resolution. It doesn't even mean the resolution has to be happy or optimistic or morally right, and the narrator doesn't have to be reliable — you can have a narrator who lies to you, the reader — but you do have to have a problem upon which to hang your hat. Part of creating the tension is conflict. A lot of it is putting your characters in a situation against all odds and in a catastrophe, despite their intentions."

There is no end to learning how to write good suspense. As in all things, the key is practice.

set your timer

Do you have a list in your notebook headed "Crises"? If not, make that list now. Crises you survived. That winter you learned your brother had stolen all of your mother's money. Hearing the diagnosis — autism — for your firstborn. When you learned the reason the credit cards were maxed out was because your husband had been calling phone sex lines.

Pick one of them and write about it in as much detail as you can. Begin in the middle of things. Don't resort to summary; don't tell us that it happened — show us. See if you can chart a course from the calm to the center of the cyclone and back out again.

Let it sit overnight — imagine soaking beans for soup — then read it over with a cool eye. Does it begin slowly and quickly accelerate? How did the people involved become so enmeshed? What do they need and what are the obstacles to that need?

If you'd prefer to do this with fictional characters, start with some favorites from your reading or even historical figures. Choose two who appeal to you, put them in a room, and set them at cross-purposes. Keep writing and see what happens. When in doubt, be outrageous — and have fun.

We speak naturally but spend
all our lives trying to write naturally.
—Margaret Wise Brown

voice and style

V oice is what distinguishes writers from one another. A compelling story and characters you want to follow are vital, but for many readers, the author's voice makes all the difference. It's what draws you to certain authors, makes you want to drink in their books, and savor the worlds they create.

When a work has a distinct voice, you know who wrote it without seeing the author's name on the cover. Voice is a signature, a stamp. It's what you come to sooner or later, if you write long enough.

As I write this chapter, I'm in a Chris Bohjalian phase. I didn't read *Midwives* when the rest of the country read it along with Oprah. I came across the book a year ago, and after I did, I read his latest, *The Buffalo Soldier*, and had him on my show. Then I read his second book, *The Law of Similars*, and an earlier work, *Trans-Sister Radio*. Now I'm on *Water Witches*, and his book of nonfiction, *Idyll Banter*, just arrived from his publisher in advance of his reappearance on my show.

All of his books that I've read are set in Vermont, my favorite state, and he explores subject matter I'm interested in: midwives, homeopathy, how people deal with tragedy. But it's his voice that makes me want to read on and on.

I believe everyone has her own voice; you just have to learn to let it shine through. It was a physiology class in college that propelled me into a writing class. I turned in a paper on the fertility drug Clomid, and the instructor, Dr. John, did not mince words when he said, "None of this sounds like it's in your voice. You might want to take a writing class."

Voice? A writing class? Hmm.

The next semester I signed up for a writing class with Marc Estrin, who, as it happened, published his first novel, *Insect Dreams*, in 2002. He had us do writing exercises and gave us assignments. My stuff was horrible; it was abstract, distanced, clichéd.

Still, I continued on with the class and kept working at it. Days before the final paper was due, I still had no idea what to write about. I hadn't even begun, but I feared that Marc might say my work was no good and I should forget all about writing. My bulky Underwood typewriter reproached me from the makeshift desk on which it sat. I warily eyed the gray hulk and the blank paper that curled from under the platen.

When I finally sat down, I found myself writing about beginning to write. I wrote about learning to tap the creative vein, how it made my teeth hurt, my bones ache, and how if I could give words to my thoughts and feelings, anybody could. When Marc handed my paper back, he said he liked it and told me I had broken through and found my voice. Voice. There was that word again. I didn't know what it meant but it sounded like it was a good thing and this inspired me. I didn't think in terms of being a writer and publishing. I was excited because I had permeated a mysterious membrane of some sort, had written something my teacher liked, words that he said sounded like me. Nothing compared. Mornings, I woke up refreshed. Depression had lifted. I wouldn't know it for some time, but I had found my calling.

Voice is a skill you work at developing. "A writer's natural voice comes from practice, from writing a lot, and trusting that you have something to say," says author Harriet Rubin, a former Doubleday editor. "When I was an editor, I would advise my authors to write about a subject they didn't have the answers to, because in the struggle to understand themselves, a voice would emerge."

Mystery writer Martha C. Lawrence told my radio audience: "Voice is the key to what makes a reader keep reading. Fresh, original, compelling voice. [It's] not something you can pick up from a weekend seminar or a writer's helpful hints column. [It's] something you have to earn through living and writing, trial and error."

When I asked Alix Kates Shulman about finding her voice, she said, "The writer just writes as she must. Sometimes as I'm writing certain scenes, I know this is good and I am in the grip of some lyrical thing beyond me, and I go with it. But those moments are rare. More of the time it's a matter of rewriting, refining, trying to get closer to what I was trying to get across, and cutting, cutting, cutting, getting down to the essence of the scene."

An easygoing style and casual voice may look simple at first glance but still require a heap of work on the part of the author. When Carolyn See, *Washington Post* book reviewer and author of *Making a Literary Life,* came on *Writers on Writing,* I asked about her breezy style.

"I want my style to be easy so that I'm not beating people over the head with how much I know," she said, "but the downside of that is people take you at your face value and give it the easy read and see the colloquial style and they think, 'Ah, a slangy moron.' Well, that's their problem."

Your unique observations and your own singular writing style go into making up your voice. Allowing your voice to come through may at first make you uncomfortable. But if you go with it, if you write as you talk or as you see things, your true voice will emerge. Voice is very much tied to language. Certain authors write for language, love playing with words and crafting sentences. Yet, writing for language doesn't mean you use words that send everybody running to the dictionary.

"Be simple," says Jacquelyn Mitchard. "Read things that are written simply and well. Mark Twain said no book worth its salt would be un-understandable to an intelligent thirteen-year-old. I believe that. I don't subscribe to the modern theory that the sentence has to be so convoluted and complicated and weighted with metaphor and complexity that it has to be read again and again for the reader to understand it. If you find yourself being carried away by the beauty of your own prose, remind yourself to be simple."

As you pay attention to writing styles, you will learn that different writers approach language differently. Robert Stone says he hears a rhythm in his head. "I feel like I'm a musician, and I have to trust my ear. As you get older, you have attacks of doubt, but you have to have confidence in your ear. It influences style. Mine came from a lot of early influences. I think I've put those influences behind me. And the style I write with is now mine. At this point, as I'm in my sixties, I see whatever influences that were on me are on younger writers. I worked my style out because it was congenial to me, because in a way, it *was* me. It's the sound of my cerebration, it's the sound of my getting loose and crazy over something, my pursuing some notion, some line of thought, some image, some landscape, and doing it in a way that I think is beautiful and doing it in a way that I think sounds right because I do believe that sound is everything."

Grammar maven Constance Hale, author of *Sin and Syntax*, says you've got to find the right pitch. "Everything consigned to the page needs to ring true. Keep your audience in mind, especially when you are setting style and tone; don't talk to readers as if they are strangers, or as if they are beneath you. To find the right pitch is to be human, to have a sense of the street while still reaching for the lofty."

Your own writing style may not be what you had hoped for when you imagined yourself as a writer. Perhaps you wanted to sound like Dorothy Parker or Virginia Woolf or F. Scott Fitzgerald. You're not alone—but eventually you've got to love the voice you've been given.

T. Jefferson Parker says he spent more time than he cares to remember emulating his writing heroes, but "sooner or later, you realize it's easier to sound like yourself than someone else."

set your timer

Read aloud. It's the best way to hear when writing is working or not. Choose a few books, essays, stories, passages, or poems you particularly like written by someone else.

Now read your own writing aloud. Sentences should have a beat, and that beat is never more apparent than when read aloud. Reading your own work aloud may be uncomfortable at first. Do it anyway. Read your work aloud whenever possible, or read it into a tape recorder, if you like, and play it back. Notice passages that work wonderfully and others that are clunkers. You may not have noticed the clunkers, had you not read them aloud.

Now, fix the image and voice of a particular author in mind, as well as his or her usual theme or subject matter, and write five hundred words as if you were that writer. Use the word choices he or she would use.

Next, think of another writer, and rewrite what you just wrote in that person's voice.

Finally, write it as *you* would write it.

Notice the power of word choices, how a small shift can change everything.

> *I think knowing what you cannot do is*
> *more important than knowing what you can do.*
> —Lucille Ball

play to your strength

What aspect of writing do you do well? Do you write great dialogue? Are you a natural storyteller? Do you write landscape description well or have an uncanny ability to capture telling details about people?

Do you even know? You may not—for some time, anyway.

A. Scott Berg, author of *Kate Remembered* and *Max Perkins: Editor of Genius*, says he had many weaknesses and few strengths when he started out.

"My strengths were in gathering material, researching, and interviewing skills. My weaknesses...where to begin? I did what most beginning writers do: I imitated my favorite writers. When I wrote about Fitzgerald, I wrote these leafy paragraphs; when I wrote about Hemingway, it was short simple sentences. It was just a mess. When my editor, Tom Congdon, began to edit what was my third or fourth draft of *Max Perkins*, he circled an entire paragraph and said, 'You know who this sounds like? Nobody! This is your voice! Write like that.' The lightbulb went off."

So what should you do—press toward your strengths and do more of what you do really well, or focus on weaknesses?

Novelist and short story writer Aimee Bender says, "Push toward your strengths because if you can exaggerate your strengths, that push toward yourself is a movement toward voice. There's something really core about the idea of writers discovering their voice. You go toward what you love about reading and you go toward what you love in your own writing. And once you get more confident at that, you take on the things that are harder, the things you're not as good at, because it will expand the breadth of your work. But there's a time for that and if you go to it at the wrong time, you almost spread yourself too thin. You don't want to dilute what is the natural bent of your work."

New writers almost always want to do what they're not that great at, perhaps imagining that real writers can do everything. It's not true. No writer does it all.

"As you go along, if you're going to continue and become a professional, you will identify the things you can do and the things you can't do," says Kate Braverman. "I was really a poet who could write dialogue. Conventional narrative has always been a weak point for me, so I learned to deal with strengths, which are language and sensory detail. I worked on those things and developed a capacity to sustain, the stamina.

"Find out what you can do, do it until you drop—you'll probably have to learn a few other things—and stay away from what you can't do."

Writing is not a triathlon. You don't have to master each writing skill or technique, no matter what your high school teachers and college professors told you. Because of spelling programs on the computer, you (unfortunately) don't even have to spell well to be a writer these days. How's that for freedom?

set your timer

You need to know what you do well. If you don't know, sit down for fifteen minutes and write a few paragraphs on what you *think* you do well, being as specific as possible, or make a list: "I hear dialogue in my head and I write it down as I hear it." "I love to create characters and feel they come alive on the page."

Then take what you consider one of your best pieces of writing and show your writing buddy or your writing group. Ask what they think your strong points are. Where their opinions and yours converge is where your strengths lie.

Press on with your strengths. Don't veer away from them until you feel confident enough to undertake a new challenge. If narrative is your strong suit, when you write a story, make it narrative heavy. If it's dialogue, write as much dialogue as you can.

Play to your strength. And your strengths will nourish you.

I write in the first person because I have always
wanted to make my life more interesting than it was.
—Diane Wakoski, Trilogy

point of view

Time and again my students—well-read, bright, talented
people—experience confusion over point of view (POV). POV
is one of the most perplexing aspects of writing fiction to understand
and do consistently. It has everything to do with how your story is
told, and how the reader *connects* with what you've written, especially with your narrator.

When I started writing, I wrote all my stories in the first person.
Even if the story wasn't about *me*, it was the easiest way to get into
storytelling mode. When I tried third person, the narrator sounded
and felt so distant. Yet, for others, the first person is *too* close or too
limited. For them, the third person works perfectly.

A refresher: First-person point of view means you use *I*. You *are*
the character speaking. You are as snug in the narrator's shoes as you
can be: *"I went to the Ringo concert and it was awesome."* Third-
person POV offers the "he" or "she" perspective: *"He went to the
Ringo concert and said it was awesome."*

Judith Ryan Hendricks writes her novels in first-person present tense, although she feels experienced authors look down on first person, thinking it the beginner's POV. Yet, for her, "It's more natural to tell the story in the present tense. You can get away with saying a lot of things that you can't if it's told in the third-person past tense."

In first person, you may be more able to get the tone of the character's voice just right because it's not filtered through a third-person narrator. You also have more access to the thoughts, feelings, and motivations of your narrator.

Kate Braverman also prefers first person. She says, "It seems more immediate to me, more modern. If you're concerned primarily with experience and sensory data and consciousness, first person is a logical choice. And I just do it better. If you naturally ice-skate, why ski?"

If you choose third-person POV, you have to decide what type of third person works for your story. One choice is *omniscient*, in which you have total knowledge of the thoughts of all of your characters and you get to play God, moving in and out of however many characters' POVs as you wish. But you aren't bound by moving in and out of the minds of your characters. You can tell more than they know and reflect, judge, and express truths and opinions as you do so. Ann Patchett's *Bel Canto* is a lovely example of this POV.

Then there is third-person subjective, or a limited third-person POV. In this POV, the story is told through the eyes of no more than a few characters. You can move in and out of those characters, writing closely, not looking down as God, but placing yourself in your characters' shoes and telling the story from the third person. For example, "Each morning when Clara awoke, she leaned in close to Wade, breathed him in and felt his arms, just to make sure he was still alive. Too many men in her family had died in their sleep and even though he had just turned forty, this was her overwhelming fear, that he might die, too." So many novelists do close third person well; several examples that come to mind are Chris Bohjalian's *The Buffalo Soldier*, Ian McEwan's *Enduring Love*, Barbara Kingsolver's *Prodigal Summer*.

Second person, which is hardly used, thrusts the reader directly into the story by using the second-person pronoun, *you*: "*You're hungry and yearning for a scone but it contains flour and sugar, and you've given up flour and sugar—for now.*" Jay McInerney uses the second person in his bestselling novel, *Bright Lights, Big City*, and does it well, but it's difficult to do and hard to get used to. Perhaps writers choose this POV because they enjoy the challenge. For vicarious thrill seekers, this can be exciting and immediate; other readers may resent the intrusion. Second person must be handled carefully.

Treat point of view seriously and give it thought before you begin writing. Novelist Jodi Picoult believes writers should be keenly aware of point of view and plan ahead to decide what POV is best for a particular piece.

"Point of view is one of the great overlooked pieces of teaching writing," says Picoult. "We always hear about the third-person objective point of view and then we hear about the first-person point of view. But there's that third-person *subjective* point of view where you can swoop in and out of characters' heads and I find that fascinating. What's even more interesting is trying to figure out which point of view you need to tell your story because, for example, if you use a first-person narrator and they aren't in the critical scene of your book, well, you're out of luck because there's nobody to tell you what's happening. So you need to think point of view through or you're going to find yourself with three hundred pages that have all been a waste.

"Third-person subjective allows you to get closer to your reader than a third-person objective point of view. It's traditional for new writers to write in third-person objective, where you're looking down at all your little figurines and you're moving them around, 'cause it's easiest. First person is the closest you can get to a character. When you take it back to a third-person subjective, it's a little more removed, it's like you're looking through a smoky window; you can see [your characters] pretty well, but there's still a plate of glass between you. When you move to third-person objective you're up in the sky looking down at what's happening."

When you're deciding what point of view to use, there are a few things to keep in mind: Do you want your readers to feel as if they are in your narrator's shoes or even yours? Do you want to write from only one character's perspective? Or, are you writing an essay? Choose first person.

Just so you don't panic, know that you're not married to whichever point of view you begin with. Authors have been known to switch POV, especially when what they're writing doesn't flow as it should.

As for switching POV, until you feel confident and in control of your writing, don't change POV midstream. If you are writing a novel that you want to write from multiple POVs, use chapter breaks to switch POV. Please don't switch in the middle of a chapter—even if you must relate interior information, and even if your favorite authors do this. It's way too abrupt. Your reader will feel as though she is watching a Ping-Pong game.

ஒ set your timer

When you read, pay attention to POV and see if you can figure out why the author chose that particular POV. And before you begin writing, dawdle a bit. Think. Ponder. Which POV works best for the piece you're about to begin?

Take a scene from something you've already written and swap POV. If you wrote it in the first person, switch it to the third; if it's in the third, switch it to the first. What happens? Does it change for better or for worse?

I have done this to entire chapters, for the good. Suddenly a piece that felt too distant now pulls in close, or a piece that was too close has the necessary remove from the reader.

Sometimes readers — and writers — confuse the author with the fictive narrator when encountering the first-person point of view. This exercise invites you to explore first person from a different perspective. Imagine that you wake up and there's someone else in bed — and that someone is *you*, or was you. Overnight you've been transformed: You are now a different gender, a different race or class, or even an animal or an insect (think Kafka). Set your timer for fifteen minutes and get to know yourself. Take a moment to become acquainted with your new physique. What is it like to be you?

Describe what it's like to be in this new body as you go about your day: If you work, how do people treat you? If you stay at home, what is that like? How do your children treat you? Let yourself go with it. Allow yourself to write recklessly, badly even, but include as much minute detail as you possibly can.

*I think Hemingway's titles should be awarded
first prize in any contest. Each of them is a poem,
and their mysterious power over readers contributes to
Hemingway's success. His titles have a life of their own,
and they have enriched the American vocabulary.*
—Sylvia Beach, bookstore owner,
Shakespeare and Company

titles: the port of entry

A title can make the difference between a reader picking up a book or passing it by. Your title is the first impression you make, and you want it to be a good one, especially when it comes to agents and editors, those pivotal people who will take on your book—or not.

Coming up with a great title is wretched. Sometimes I think it's the worst part of writing. It can make you pull hair from your poor head.

The title for this book began as "Writing Like There's No Tomorrow." For several years I taught a writing workshop with that name and thought it worked for a book title. But, in the end, it sounded too doom and gloom. It actually scared some people. So I changed it to "Write This Moment." It was getting warmer, but it still wasn't quite right. When I hit on *Pen on Fire*, I knew that was it. It expressed the essence of the book. Finding this title took years—literally. But when a title works just right, that's it. You'll know it when you've found a title that sticks.

Sometimes you find a title hidden in the text, a phrase or a word that screams out, "I'm your title!" Literary agent Sandra Dijkstra said that when she took on Amy Tan, author of *The Joy Luck Club*, the book's title was "Wind and Water." Dijkstra says she was concerned that coming from an unknown agent in California, that title would get her laughed out of New York City. When she read through Tan's pages, she came upon the phrase "Joy Luck Club" to describe a social club Amy's parents belonged to in which they discussed stocks and finances with friends.

"I got goose bumps and asked Amy if I could use that title," says Dijkstra. "She assented, although to her, these words simply represented 'my parents' club.' Amy left for China with her mom, and I went off to New York with her pages, now titled 'Joy Luck Club.' Once editors read Amy's irresistible pages, framed by this alluring title, everyone bid, and I had an auction running."

The title is too important to people's perceptions of a work to get it wrong. Authors often think the title can be changed later; it can be and often is. But a good title serves as the entryway into the work, and, as Dijkstra says, "It is the gateway to the author's mind, the first thing an editor knows about how you write."

I'm fascinated with how authors come up with titles. Carolyn Parkhurst, author of *The Dogs of Babel*, says, "[Dogs] was a working title at first, but I liked it as a symbol of lack of communication. The book is about Paul's inability to communicate with this dog he's trying to teach to talk and it's also about the inability to communicate with the people we're closest to. There's also in the title the story of Babel, this element of hubris, of trying to get above yourself in the natural order of things, which is very much what Paul is doing. By trying to teach a dog to talk, he's going into territory maybe he shouldn't go into. It's coming out in England under the title *Lorelei's*

Secret. They didn't like *The Dogs of Babel*; they all thought it sounded like a thriller. It's an interesting cultural thing; in some ways, it's a marketing decision."

Sometimes authors carry titles with them for years before they use them. The title and title story of Aimee Bender's first book, *The Girl in the Flammable Skirt,* came to her years before she started writing stories that would find their way into the book.

"There was a recall for flammable skirts at a store where I was in the checkout line with a friend buying a shirt, and it immediately hit me as an image I liked. I thought I would like to have that as a book title someday. I held on to it for years, hoping it would fit."

Claire Tristram submitted her first novel to an agent with the working title "Changiz and Pilar." He took her on, but before he sent her book to editors, he changed the title to "Anonymous Sex." When he sold it to Farrar, Straus, Giroux, the title changed again.

"The editor changed it immediately to "An American Affair" before circulating it in-house for comments," says Tristram. "That title didn't find favor, either, so the editor asked me for a list of one-name titles from which to choose. I thought of about twenty." They finally settled on *After,* and the book was published in May 2004.

Tristram says, "The title was more or less the last thing to be decided in the process, even after edits were done. Although After was one of my choices on the list I submitted, it was somewhere in the middle of a long list. I don't think I would have come up with it if it had been solely up to me to figure out a title, but now I love it and think it's perfect. As author, I was given veto power over any title choice, but it was very much a group process to come up with the final result, rather than my individual inspiration."

Ron Carlson says, "I tell students, when in doubt, to title their story after the smallest concrete object in the story. I warn them off of plays on words ('The Rent Also Rises'—no; 'Life in My Cat House'—no) and no grand reaches either: 'Reverence,' 'Respect,'

'Regret,' 'Greed,' 'Adventure,' 'Retribution.' And never use the worst title of all time: 'The Gift,' a story I read six times a year."

set your timer

Study titles — of magazine articles, short stories, novels, nonfiction books. Which grab you and why? Titles that pique your interest but are either not easily deciphered or that have multiple meanings are good choices. Of the works you read, can you see why the authors titled them as they did? What does the title tell you about the book? Which would you retitle?

Set your timer and explore how these titles do or don't work. And come up with your own list of titles. Keep them somewhere to be used later. Sometimes a title can jump-start a piece of work, too.

*Begin with an individual and you find
that you have created a type; begin with a type
and you find that you have created — nothing.*
—F. Scott Fitzgerald

character building

I f you want interesting fictional characters, give them personal contradictions. The most interesting people you know have internal contradictions, so why shouldn't your characters? It's easy enough to get stuck creating characters who are perfect, but in fiction, as in life, perfection is boring. A character who never falters, who never contradicts herself, who is just too nice, leaves the reader cold. Conversely, characters at odds with themselves or their surroundings, who are fraught by internal contradictions, create conflict, and conflict is what drives a page-turner.

It's the characters who have bad hair days, who've lost a parent or a child, who struggle to pay bills, who need to lose a few pounds, who love humanity but can't stand people, that intrigue us and keep us reading.

Where do complex, contradictory, believable characters come from? Your own life and the people you've known, for one.

Elizabeth George says that every one of her chance encounters and relationships provides the seed for the characters in her novels. "Not that I put the people I've known in novels," she says, "but I use aspects of them a lot. A man's fear of commitment, a woman's need for external perfection, a mother/daughter dispute. I never plan to use them, but when I'm sitting at my computer doing stream of consciousness writing, a character evolves. I've only had one person recognize himself."

Ayelet Waldman and Michael Chabon mingle family life and fiction freely. Waldman says, "I take little bits of all sorts of people—myself, my family, people on the street. It's how I try to make sure my characters are real, by basing them in different ways on different real people. And as of yet, neither Michael nor I have discovered a dead body, but other parts of the Juliet books are pretty true to our lives together."

Chabon also borrows from actual experience, but he is not above playing with the reader's propensity to blur the line between the author and the narrator: "I frequently will draw on a lot of different things, as I need them, bits and pieces of stuff I've experienced, people that I've known. As actual details of my life have become more known to more people, I've explored that relationship between my life and my fiction. The last story I wrote is about a father and a son, and I have a son—plenty of people know my son is the same age as the character I'm writing about—and I very deliberately played with the fact that readers wouldn't be sure whether they were reading about me or something I was making up. I tried to write this short story in a very matter-of-fact tone, as if I were reporting an incident from my life and yet, really the incident and events were almost entirely invented."

"Everybody assumes it's all your life, anyway," says Waldman. "That makes it extra fun to make stuff up."

But characters do come from the imagination; by combining

characteristics that interest you or that contrast with one another, you'll come up with a character unique unto herself. Regarding characters, T. Jefferson Parker says, "I just make them up. Typically, they represent or embody some fairly simple combinations of human characteristics."

Regardless of where they come from, you must know your characters. "You have to know who they really are," says Iris Rainer Dart, author of *Beaches*. "You have to be able to get inside their brains."

One caveat: Don't fall so in love with your characters that you protect them. You must have compassion for them, yet the most compelling characters experience danger of some sort—emotional, physical, or financial.

"You have to create characters you like and then beat them up," says Janet Fitch.

The most interesting people and characters are not two-dimensional, but multidimensional. Nice, magnanimous people are great to have as friends, but in fiction, they make for flat characters.

Think of the fictional characters that stay with you; often they're memorable because of their conflicting purposes or the way they play against the stereotype. Some characters that come to mind include a Japanese businessman passionate for opera (*Bel Canto*); a logical, science-minded lawyer who seeks a homeopathist for treatment (*The Law of Similars*); a compelling TV talk-show host who falls in love with a facially deformed police detective (*Silent Joe*). The best characters do the unexpected or embody unpredictable traits. It's their internal contradictions that make them fascinating and keep a reader's interest.

set your timer

One way to create characters is to do their "bone structure," as Lagos Egri described in his classic, *The Art of Dramatic Writing*. Take your notebook and sit somewhere comfy to brainstorm. Write your character's name at the top of the page and write the words (so you remember): *physical, psychological,* and *sociological.* For fifteen minutes, write about your character.

Under the heading "Physical," write about what your character looks like, childhood diseases, current medical conditions, and anything else that physically describes her.

Under "Psychological," write about your character's psychological and emotional makeup: how she feels about relationships, her approach to life, what she dreams, how she treats herself and others.

Under "Sociological," write about your character's upbringing, what school she went to, what she majored in at college (if she went to college), where she works, what sort of music she listens to, her favorite movies, her best friends.

By the time you're done with this, you should know all you need to know to get started. When you reach an impasse in a work of fiction, you can go back to your character's bone structure, and know what she'd do.

You can also get close to a character by having your character write a letter to someone in her own voice. For fifteen minutes, have your character talk about things that only the recipient of the letter would know about. Have it be a long letter—long enough to allow you to get to know your character's concerns.

And when a person's quirky quality strikes you, be sure to jot it down in your notebook. You never know when that personality trait is just what you'll need to flesh out a character.

Compassion is the basis of morality.
—Arthur Schopenhauer

compassion 101

When you first decide you want to write, you take classes on plotting, outlining, structure, creating characters, writing short stories, beginning and ending your novel, and revising and selling your fiction. Yet, there's a class you won't find included in the curriculum of any writing program I know of. It's on how you need compassion and empathy to become a great writer.

Janet Fitch, author of *White Oleander*, said she had to develop compassion to become a better writer. When she came on my radio show, she talked about the most important thing she ever told her students.

"I had to become a better person," she said. "When I started writing, I was pretty snotty. I'd go for the cheap laugh. I had to grow up, develop more compassion for other people, feel more for the human predicament."

Compassion also figures in when you want to create a good villain. The best writers seem to know and love all their characters, even the villains — *especially* the villains sometimes. Tell me Thomas Harris didn't love Hannibal Lecter, the charismatic psychopath in *Silence of the Lambs*. He had to love him to be able to endow such a creepy character with depth and appeal. And Gollum in *Lord of the Rings* is such a compelling villain because he has a streak of something more complex than sheer villainy; he's a classic example of a character at odds with himself. Ann Patchett avoided stereotypes and gave the terrorists in *Bel Canto* complex personalities, endowing them with an unexpected richness and depth.

Crime writer Robert Ferrigno agrees. "Compassion and empathy are a rarely mentioned but critical component of good writing in general, and thriller writing in particular," he says. "I work very hard at creating villains that are real, that are human beings rather than puppets manipulated by the author in furtherance of a plot requirement. The author being empathic accomplishes this. Observe people in real life, asking oneself who they are, how they got that way, what do they eat for breakfast, what television shows do they watch, what jokes or situations do they laugh at? I'm quite serious about this. You need to get inside your character/villain, which is the purest definition of empathy, to get inside them and feel what they are feeling now and what they felt before. The writer must know the backstory of every character, even if the backstory doesn't figure directly into the printed page. My villains have soul because I don't believe in monsters."

Ron Carlson says, "The most undervalued craft device that fiction writers need is empathy. You need to be able to actually imagine what your characters are going through. You've got to stay close. When you're in a story and dealing with people you're not certain of or you've just come to meet because they stepped into your story, it's very important to go slow and sit in their chair."

If you don't feel deeply for all of your characters and the situation they're in, there's a good chance no one else will either. You gave them life. Now give them depth. After all, writing — especially writing fiction — is about putting yourself in someone else's shoes.

✍ set your timer

As Carlson also says, you don't have to love the people or the characters you write about, but they should be at least as smart as you. Look beyond stereotypes.

Pick someone to write about who really bothers you, perhaps someone who makes a nuisance of themselves—a brash teenager who speeds down your street playing music at top volume that you hate, your next-door neighbor whose cigar smoke wafts through your open window, a woman in your condo complex who lavishes attention on her cats but just about runs you down if you happen to cross in front of her car.

Set your timer for fifteen minutes and write a description of one or more of these people. And here's the challenge: Do it without turning them into caricatures. Look beyond the surface. Does the teenager have a little sister he dotes on? Does the next-door neighbor play the cello beautifully? Why does the woman in the condo complex prefer animals to people, and what does it mean for her to love something? Those particulars, the fascinations, interests, and complexities of all people, even those who bother you, are the things to keep in mind when delineating character. Try freewriting from the point of view of the person you've chosen.

Also consider someone who's made the six o'clock news. Write his backstory: What was his childhood like? How was he treated by parents, teachers, and schoolmates? Did he have nasty siblings? A house-confining illness, or an all-too-obvious physical flaw he was chastised for as a kid? Knowing your characters' backstories is important because it influences their take on life and the choices they make.

If you have trouble doing this exercise, take a look at your own attitude toward yourself. Try giving a fictional character a quality of your own that you abhor. Writing can be a journey to self-discovery; if something bothers you about someone else, most likely this is a quality that you share on some level.

Plunge deeply into human nature and not only will your writing improve, you might, like Janet Fitch, find yourself a better person for having done so.

Always get to the dialogue as soon as possible.
—P. G. Wodehouse

say what? writing dialogue

Good dialogue isn't just conversation recorded. It's a distillation of the spoken word that cuts to the quick, leaving out the fillers that punctuate everyday speech, such as the "um's" and "like's" and "you know's" and the mundane phrases and social niceties that are necessary in life but a bore in fiction.

Instead of "She picked up the phone and said, 'How are you?'" what about "She picked up the phone and heard her mother's voice before she even said hello: 'Honey, your brother's missing.'" Good dialogue starts at an active, involved place and makes you want to read on to know more.

There's nothing better than good dialogue to show us who characters are by revealing their quirks and traits and motivations. Good dialogue can kick a story into high gear, helping a scene progress and teaching us something we didn't know about the characters or the plot.

Although dialogue is more — and less — than a transcription of conversation, make an effort to listen to people's conversations, noting the way things are said as well as what is said. Every writer should spend some time as an eavesdropper. It's a guilty pleasure and an invaluable source of material.

You'll know good dialogue when you hear it. When you're out on a walk, at a restaurant, or at the market, and you find yourself leaning in to hear more, you know it's because the dialogue you're hearing is smokin'! I was at the Long Beach flea market, walking down an aisle between tables of carnival glass, old windows, and vintage fabrics when I overheard a woman say: "How about this for the name of an insect: queenie white thighs?" Later someone else said, "Didn't we buy an iguana here?" I got out my notebook and jotted these lines down.

There is so much to say about writing dialogue and whole books have been written on the topic. What you'll find here are a few salient points.

When you write fiction, one of your most important decisions is whether dialogue or narration works best for a particular scene. Too often dialogue is used to provide information that could better be given indirectly. Think about pacing. Narration speeds things along by condensing speech or slows it down by offering long descriptive passages. It tends to tell the reader what is happening; dialogue dramatizes that action, showing not telling. Dialogue also breaks up the rhythm of long narrative stretches, livening the writing by letting the characters speak for themselves.

Paradoxically, dialogue, coupled with gestures, is often useful in getting across what isn't said in talking around something. It draws the reader in, forcing her to pay close attention and interpret or anticipate the course of the narrative. For instance, a couple sits at the breakfast table. "You've seemed distant lately," one partner says to the other, who is engrossed in the newspaper. She doesn't look up, but says, "I've just been busy. Everything's fine." But *is* everything fine? The only way to find out is to read on.

I asked my student Phil Doran, once a TV sitcom writer (for *The Wonder Years*, among other shows) and now an author, for his suggestions on writing dialogue.

"I try to 'hear' my characters speak because dialogue is about the spoken word," he says, "and that's why reading dialogue aloud is a handy thing to do. Like real dialogue, it is unstructured and free-flowing. People speak in sentence fragments and cut each other off. And if I'm not going for what you'd consider a joke, which is mostly what I am going for, I at least try to find a spike somewhere in the run that contains something shocking, or revealing. In other words, what is there in this run of dialogue that makes it worth doing, as opposed to giving the same information in a paragraph?"

Short story master Ron Carlson elaborates further. "The bad dialogue you see isn't the old clunky dialogue we used to see a long time ago, real wooden and kind of telling. The bad dialogue you see now is a little blasé and a little television. I was watching television last week and within thirty-five minutes I heard the line, 'I can't believe you...' whatever it was. TV writers should post a rule that anyone who says that will be fined.

"They say dialogue is meant to advance a story. Well, it is if the story is *The Da Vinci Code*, but it isn't if it's one of my stories. The dialogue *may* advance the story, but it's going to have trouble since the characters don't know the story yet and they've got to sit there and find it out. I listen as hard as I can to them and I try to let them speak to their ability. Not everybody knows or is able to articulate their current state. Dialogue is not meant to be on topic; it's meant to be dramatic, personal. It comes from the source, the heart. So many times when you're writing dialogue, you're really writing the way people *don't* talk to each other, the way we *can't* listen to each other, or the way we use words to obtrude, to obscure and hide.

"What we [readers] are looking for is somebody that so obviously has thought about every word, the way Annie Proulx does or Annie Dillard, two writers who are real fresh. I think Robert Stone does. [In their work] you never see these big clunky blocks of prose that the people use when they start to get painted in the corner."

Good dialogue tends to be streamlined, minimal. To the point, but rarely right on the nose. Good dialogue runs along parallel lines, intersecting now and then.

Just a few more details:

In most types of writing — except for romance novels — use *said* (if you're in past tense) and *says* (if you're in present) as attributions. Occasionally, use *asked, recalled,* or similar under-the-top verbs. This is one area where active, descriptive verbs should be avoided. Never use attributions like *carped, retorted, whined, exclaimed, chortled,* or *vomited* (unless you're going for humor or writing a children's book). These tags draw attention to themselves and not to the words being spoken. Forms of *said* are as invisible in a line of dialogue as the wind.

Consider using action to show who's talking: "'There's nothing sexier than a man who cooks.' Liz ran her fingers down Chris's back as he stirred the applesauce."

A dim-witted character's dialogue is unbearable. So is most dialogue written phonetically.

Let your characters interrupt one another.

Get caught up in the rhythm of speech. "Remember that [dialogue's] a stylization, not a literal version of the way people actually talk," says crime writer T. Jefferson Parker.

And read your work aloud. Reading aloud allows you to hear the glitches and smooth them out.

set your timer

Here's a writing assignment: Go to a café or restaurant, one with the tables situated close to one another so you can hear conversations around you, or go to a restaurant by the off-ramp of a freeway where travelers from all over stop to eat and rest and gab. Find a spot and just listen and take notes.

Pay attention to what you hear. Listen to the cadences of conversation as well as what is said. Speed, interruptions, phrases such as "I think" or "It's just my opinion, but..." reveal a lot. Who interrupts who? Does one person pause before speaking? Fail to reply? How do men speak differently than women? Author and instructor Tony Eprile says he often recommends Deborah Tannen's *You Just Don't Understand*, which is about power relationships in dialogue and how men and women use dialogue differently.

Pay attention to what the people don't say, and be aware of what you don't write down. Pay attention to when you lean in, when you shush whoever is with you or curse the background music — when that happens, you know you're hearing good dialogue.

Likewise, pay attention to what doesn't interest you, the filler language that makes you start looking at the menu again or considering a piece of apple pie à la mode. Good dialogue makes you want to find out what happens next.

Now, for fifteen minutes, write your own conversation between a man and a woman. In gripping dialogue, there is often conflict, however subtle. One is saying yes while the other is saying no. What does the woman need? What does the man need?

Write it down, then revise. Embellish, delete, strengthen.

Remember to get the weather in
your damn book—weather is very important.
—Ernest Hemingway to John Dos Passos, 1932

set the stage

There are books in which setting is so vivid it's almost a character. Annie Proulx's *The Shipping News* couldn't take place anywhere but Newfoundland. Susan Straight's *Highwire Moon* is most definitely Riverside, California. And Chris Bohjalian's novels perfectly epitomize Vermont, its unique weather and landscape.

Before you start writing, consider the setting you plan to use. Why did you choose a particular location? Not every locale needs to be strikingly vivid, but verisimilitude doesn't hurt. Detailed surroundings add depth and texture to your story.

Crime writer Laura Lippman says she intentionally places her novels in Baltimore, Maryland. "I think of Baltimore in some ways—and it sounds kind of corny—as the love of my life. It's certainly the thing I've had the longest sustained relationship with as an adult, and I never cease to find it less than fascinating. The city as a whole is a real unwieldy subject so I feel as if I'm never going to run out of things to say about it."

Poet and short story writer Donald Hall, author of *Willow Temple*, says, "Place is utterly important to me. I live in a house in rural New Hampshire where my grandmother and mother were born. I came here when I was six weeks old and I only moved here full-time in 1975. The first poem I ever published when I was sixteen years old was out of this place and many, many, many of my poems, essays, stories, have to do with where I live, what I look at."

Place your story in a setting that intrigues you, one that you know well enough to show in detail. You don't have to live there or be from there, although you should at least have visited. It helps to keep a journal when you travel to draw from later. So many particulars fade away if you don't record them. I've written about India time and again, and the notes I took when I was there have helped immensely.

set your timer

I call this one "Postcard from Paradise." Set the timer and write for fifteen minutes as if you are traveling and writing to a good friend who's never been where you are. Pick a place you've been and tell your friend what it looks, sounds, feels, and smells like. If you are touring fall foliage in New England, write about the colors and the smell of fall in the countryside and the crunch of dead leaves underfoot. Stay away from words like *beautiful* or *majestic*. Use tangible, evocative details instead.

An interesting variation is to write about a place you'd like to visit, perhaps that you've read about or seen pictures of. It can be a place you've dreamed of or it can be a totally imaginary place. Create a fictional name for this place. Don't skimp on details.

I wanted to choose words that
even you would have to be changed by.
—Adrienne Rich, "Implosions"

⌘

poetry: the beautiful stepchild

Poetry has much to teach fiction and nonfiction writers. Even if you have no interest in writing poetry, read it for the sound of the language, for the rhythm of the sentences, and for the metaphors and similes.

I started studying poetry and writing it in college. Since then, I've published a little, won a contest, and still write it sporadically—usually when I'm depressed, which I'm glad to say is not too often. But I continually read it, buy books of poetry, and have poets on my show.

Frances Mayes published volumes of poetry before writing her bestselling books. "Reading poetry and writing poetry is about the best training you can give yourself for being any kind of writer," says Mayes, "whether it's writing a letter to your mother or a law brief or an article or whatever. When you study poetry, you learn about the psychology of the rhythm of language and you learn about image and repetition. All those elements you study in poetry are also elements of other writing. So when I sat down to write *Under the Tuscan*

Sun and *Bella Tuscany*, I found I was still writing poems that I had always written but I had somehow translated them into prose poems in disguise."

In *White Oleander*, you'll find poetic language on each page. Janet Fitch says, "I read a lot of poetry. Poets are the standard-bearers of language. Poets can't get by on story, they have to make it count word by word. As prose writers, we need to rise to the level of what the poets do."

Sometimes poets evolve into fiction writers. With her third published book of poetry, *Black Candle*, Chitra Divakaruni, author of *The Vine of Desire*, found her writing veering toward narrative. "I was becoming more and more interested in story and character and in showing the growth of characters and their relationship," she says. "It seemed fiction was the medium I needed to move into to allow that full expression." When you read Divakaruni's fiction, it's impossible not to see how poetry has influenced her work.

Give poetry a chance to influence your writing. If nothing else, the next time you're in the bookstore, wander over to the poetry section, randomly open books, and read a few lines. Go with what grabs you, not with what you think you *should* read. What you read should be accessible, yet somewhat mysterious. When you read a poem that attracts you, reread it, see what you experience the second or third time around. Study it for word choice, for how the poet distills language and fits an entire moment onto one page.

"The main thing you can say about poetry is that it forms a history of human emotion," says Billy Collins. "We have histories that record treaties, battles, labor disputes, and social movements, but there's only one history we have of the beating of the human heart, and that's poetry. To be connected to that is to be brought into touch with this community of feeling which forms the human past."

Poetry matters, even if you have absolutely no inclination to write it. Lynne Sharon Schwartz says, "Poetry distills. In one poem you can say what you might take a whole novel to say. Poetry is like music.

Why do we need music? It's very hard to say; it's a delight, it reminds us of things that go beyond our daily lives, it reminds us of why we want to be alive. Poetry carries the history of the language in it. If you read great poetry, either contemporary or back to Shakespeare, you can feel the language growing. So writers need to read poetry to keep a sense of the living language. People often say poets have to be a lot more careful with language than prose writers. I don't like to think that. Even as I write prose, I think of the language as sharp and as vulnerable to the touch as poets have to do. I learned that from poetry."

set your timer

Take a newspaper article, read it, then cross out every word that seems unimportant, keeping only strong nouns and verbs. Go over it again. Write down what's left and read it aloud. Are you left with the essence of the piece? Add words where you need them.

Or take a poem from a book of poetry or a magazine like the *New Yorker,* and pick one line. Write that line down. Now, build a scene around it. Freewrite for fifteen minutes, using that line as a prompt.

God hides in the details.
—Ludwig Mies van der Rohe

obsessed with detail

I relentlessly press everyone for details. I ask my husband, Brian: "What did your mom say when you gave her the necklace? What happened at the gig?"

I ask my son: "What happened at school today? What did you learn? Tell me one important thing."

I berate my students to include details in their work. "How did your character feel after she saw her house go up in flames? What was the light like, the smell?"

I'd nag the cat if he could talk: "What are you thinking? Which toy do you like best and why? Why do you wake me at 5:30 A.M. when you know I don't like it? Be specific!"

Generic answers and clichés are the stuff of small talk, not writing. A casual acquaintance who inquires about your summer vacation might well be content with "We had a really good time"; a good friend will want something more. The more particulars, the better: "We went to Wildwood, my best friends Diane Eckhart, Debbie

Wright, Sue Lacko, and I. We walked the boardwalk and ate Belgian waffles and I met Wayne Kassin, who lives in Manhattan. He dared me to get on that strange ride, the Hell Hole, with him. It spun so fast the centrifugal force pasted us to the walls, and then Wayne looked so funny plastered there with his white pants and blue and white polka-dotted shirt glowing in the black light."

Details animate life and make your writing come alive. Unless you're writing a philosophical treatise or a scholarly paper expected to be dry and rich in abstractions, your writing needs to grip the reader. One way to do that is to use the senses when creating a description of something; describe what it looked like, felt like, tasted like, or smelled like. Smell is our most primal sense and is easily overlooked in writing; smell can take us back to our early memories or evoke strong feelings and associations. The smell of certain wood smoke reminds me of India. Remember the way the house smells on a holiday when someone's been cooking all day, or the smell of the school cafeteria in the ninth grade when it was spaghetti day. Remember taste, too; all I have to do is think the word *lemon* and my salivary glands come alive.

It's the telling details you want. If you were to describe the person you're married to or the one you left behind, what would you say? How would you describe him or her? Would you call him tall, dark, and handsome? No, you wouldn't do that, because you've heard that phrase so many times you no longer know what it means, and it's a cliché. Once it was fresh; it isn't anymore. When you hear it said that someone is handsome or beautiful, can you actually visualize a specific person?

You could talk about the way his pale blue eyes rarely blink. Or perhaps how she walks with such perfect posture it appears she knows exactly where she's headed. Instead of saying he is preoccupied, describe how you know: *I catch him staring into space as he sits on the sofa in the midday light, the corners of his mouth turning slightly up like a cat's. What else could he be thinking about but his*

*son—your stepson—whom he hasn't heard from in years, since his
mother moved him out of state?*

Freewrites can be used to help you focus on particulars. Try using
a color prompt and another noncolor prompt. In one of my classes,
the words were "no white paint" and "mountain goat." Here's what
I did:

> She covered everything that came in the door with white paint.
> One night her husband came in late, beer on his breath, lip-
> stick smudging his broad pink cheeks, and he was sure she
> would pick a fight as she approached him, her eyebrows locked
> in a scowl, and the closer she got he felt himself almost cower,
> fearful of her—he had actually come to fear her!—she was so
> unpredictable these days, playing Benny Goodman or Henny
> Youngman or whoever the hell they were, at two in the morn-
> ing as she baked baklava wearing a flowery bikini from the
> seventies and rubber webbed flipper feet. Sometimes she re-
> minded him of a **mountain goat,** all scowly and fierce, and as
> she approached him he saw the paintbrush in her hand, com-
> ing at his face, landing on his face, and he yelled, **"No white
> paint,"** but it was too late. She ran the wet brush across his
> cheek, smooth and slow like a lover's tongue.

The details provide a much more vivid picture, don't they? Details bring situations and people to life.

  set your timer

Try using a color prompt along with a noncolor prompt, as I
just did, and for fifteen minutes write as detailed a scene as
you can.

Or create a still life and write about it. Walk around your
house and collect things: a lemon, three chocolate kisses, a pair

of vintage eyeglasses, a chunk of amethyst, a vase of flowers, and a ticket stub from a movie, for example. Arrange these items on the table or your desk, and freewrite for fifteen minutes, using the still life as a prompt.

You could also collect paint chips from the paint section of the hardware store and using the colors, and even the names of the colors ("Nephrite" for light aqua, "cozumel" for teal, "Flagstaff" for beige), as prompts.

Detail the senses by writing for fifteen minutes on a certain food, such as candy or popcorn, for someone who has never tasted it. Write about a visual scene for someone who can't see, and write about a piece of music for someone who can't hear.

Writing and rewriting are a
constant search for what one is saying.
—John Updike

revision

Most beginning writers—and even some experienced ones—don't much like the idea of rewriting, at least at first. Which is when I become the nagging parent: "Change your attitude!" I tell them. "You won't progress until you do." Actually, I am a little kinder than that. I administer the medicine with a spoonful of sugar or two: I tell them that once they make revision their friend, their work will soar.

One of two things then happens: They decide writing is just too damn hard and they'd rather stick to reading, or their attitude begins to adjust. Those who brace themselves learn to see that revision isn't just important—it's vital. It can make or break your writing.

Somewhere, fledgling writers mistakenly learn that coming up with great ideas is the most important thing, not rewriting. They also believe they should be able to say exactly what they mean the first time out of the gate.

Nothing else in life is like this. Who prepares a fabulous meal the first time they cook? Or plays a piano concerto at will? Or removes someone's tonsils? Even your first breath was helped along a little.

It's my guess we're so presumptuous about writing because for most of our lives we've been putting words together. It follows that many beginners believe that crafting a perfect sentence, paragraph, story, article, screenplay, or novel should be easy, and that this masterpiece will flow out of them like water from a spring. Sure, some pieces arrive more whole than others, but mostly you'll find that what you write requires a greater or lesser degree of revision.

Many novelists have rewritten manuscripts multiple times before they finally sold their book to a major publisher. Hemingway was said to have revised *For Whom the Bell Tolls* forty times. Janet Fitch says she went through *White Oleander* almost fifty. Ann Packer, author of *Dive from Clausen's Pier*, says she wrote nine complete drafts of her book over ten years. "I'd want to do another draft because people would raise questions that were interesting to me," she says. "Or conversely, you have ten people saying a scene didn't work, and you didn't know this but if ten people are saying it, it must be true. So it was a combination of being provoked to think more myself, having my eyes opened to things that weren't working, and also, it was appropriate to be revising because that's what writing is all about."

You can learn to appreciate revision, especially if you frame it like this: At least you have pages that need revising, a major accomplishment in itself. Revising may not seem as fun or as creative as writing the first draft, yet there's a distilled joy that comes from tweaking a sentence or an entire work to fulfill your original intention.

Jo-Ann Mapson believes that rewriting is the most wonderful gift a writer can receive. "For me, it's where the craft works its magic. Things slip into their slots. What isn't needed sloughs away. In my youth, I thought rewriting was a waste of time—what ego I had!"

Susan Straight loves revision. She says, "When I began writing early on, my favorite things to write were those long passages of description. We love that, the lush description where we get to use all our metaphors and things, but you realize that when you get to be forty-one and you're reading late at night, what's going to keep you moving is some sort of narrative flow as well. I send my work to my best friend, Holly, and she's really funny because she'll say to me, 'You need to cut this because you must be hungry.' What she means is, I'll have all this lush description and everything is green as boiled cabbage, or tight as a burrito, and she'll write on the page, 'Go get a snack, okay?' For me, revision is going through the novel or essay and finding all that deadwood that I had to get on the page just to know what these characters are doing. The editor I work with at NPR has been really helpful. One of my favorite things is to be on the computer and we're both on the phone, and she'll say, 'Let's cut one hundred words out of this.' It's wonderful because you see what can go and you see this spare, elegant kind of writing. In my twenties when I started out, everything was very long; I'd write these twenty-five-page short stories. I wrote four-hundred-, five-hundred-page novels. Now I really like the idea of something being simple and concise."

I've been repeating the phrase, "Writing is rewriting," for so long I no longer remember who originally said it. Keep in mind that rewriting is a wonderful opportunity; it helps you make your work the best it can be. Post the words WRITING IS REWRITING on your computer monitor or wherever you work, so you remember how good writing becomes that way.

When you're starting out, the best time to revise is after you write a first draft, not while you're writing it. Don't mess with your first chapter or scenes so many times you become sick of your story and give up on it.

"You should barrel through the first draft," says crime writer Laura Lippman. "I believe Steinbeck said that: just get through the first draft, no matter what. I once had a character change gender halfway through a manuscript. I said, 'That's okay, I'll go back for it in draft two.' By the time I came back around to those early chapters, not only would I have the right gender for my characters, but I'd have other information as well. With each subsequent draft, the characters are sharper and I hope more real to life.

"Computers are wonderful; I wouldn't work without one. But they can really mess you up if you're a perfectionist; they make it easy to *be* a perfectionist. You could spend forever on chapter one, going back into it every day, changing this word or that word. So my rule is to barrel through, to go from point *a* to point *z*, over and over again."

Edwidge Danticat, author of *Behind the Mountains,* says, "For shorter pieces, I try to do an entire draft before I revise, but in a novel, I usually revise at some point. I'll read all that I have before I continue. But I find myself revising when I'm stuck, when I can't go further, when I'm in the murderous middle, as they say."

Writing is rewriting. Accept it, and get over it.

set your timer

Put a chapter, story, or whatever you've been working on away for a few days — or weeks. Sleep on it and allow it to simmer on a subconscious level.

When you're ready to look at it again, take your piece out and read it. Better yet, read it aloud. If you're feeling especially brave, read into a tape recorder and play it back. You'll hear places that need work, words that sound contrived, sentences in which the rhythm is off.

You may revise a draft a few times or many times. Work a piece as much as you need to, until you feel there's nothing left to do. But don't work the life out of it. Another aspect of rewriting is knowing when to stop.

Once the disease of reading has laid hold upon the system it weakens it so that it falls an easy prey to that other scourge which dwells in the inkpot and festers in the quill. The wretch takes to writing.
—Virginia Woolf

you are what you read

E ven though many authors didn't write as children, most—if not all—of us read. I can still remember the thrill of arriving home from elementary school to find that a box filled with new Nancy Drew mysteries had arrived in the mail. I couldn't wait to open the carton, lift out the books, and choose one. The feel and smell of the new untouched pages was a delight. The possibilities held within those pages, the world I would enter for a time, was more exciting than going to movies. It's still that way.

If you want to be a writer you must be a reader first. Certainly you need to write, but without reading, you're leaving out an essential component of the writing life. Only by studying great writing can you even hope to approximate it.

Billy Collins says he's astounded when his new students tell him they want to write poetry but they don't want to read it. They say they want their writing to be "fresh," uninfluenced by others. He likens it to a musician going to Julliard and saying he wants to play music but doesn't listen to it.

"They'd call security!" Collins says.

"It's all in the reading," says poet Stephen Dunn. "To have read your betters and to read them with humility, to know they're far superior to you and to hold the ones who are your favorites as beacons, to try to reach toward them... if you do that, then there's a chance for you. To have absorbed what a good sentence is, to read everything, to know how a poem or a certain poet moves down the page... that kind of alertness comes from serious reading."

Many of us didn't find our way to serious reading until we went to college. In high school, most of us were too rebellious or confused or just too young to know that reading is about more than fulfilling an assignment. We're encouraged to read books we can't relate to; the classics are wonderful and a fundamental aspect of our education as writers, but in high school, the classics can do more harm than good—especially if we're not also encouraged to read the books that suit our teenage psyches. Having to read *Anna Karenina* in high school may feel more like punishment than a treat, whereas when you're in college, or later, you're ready to appreciate Tolstoy's language, depth of plot, and character development.

Even if you're working on nonfiction, it's still important—even vital for your life as a writer—to read fiction and poetry. Author Amy Bloom says, "I don't even know what to say about writers who don't read fiction. Why the hell not? Nothing to be learned from Tolstoy, Chekhov, Shakespeare, Alice Munro, Nick Hornby, or Willa Cather? How could that be? I read a lot of poetry because it puts such emphasis on the succinct and present image (as good journalism does, I think). Poetry also shakes things up inside, leaps over narrative and stirs the pond."

As writers, we are the sum of our reading and our experience. How can we know good writing unless we read it and imbibe it? Just as the food we eat goes to make up our physical selves, our reading makes up our writing selves. Eat junk food, the body suffers. Read trash, the writing suffers.

Read all sorts of things, especially in your preferred genre. If you want to write literary fiction, read literary fiction. Mysteries — read them. Articles? Stock up on magazines and pore through them. Children's books? Gobble them up. Absorb, study, pick up techniques, notice how the author uses point of view and voice. Study various writers for different reasons: read Virginia Woolf for the clarity of her prose; read Elmore Leonard for his use of dialogue. Underline original similes and metaphors. Take note. Pay attention. And then sit down yourself, and write.

"Every now and then I'll be reading something — and it's fairly rare, I think, for most writers, to leap up and want to write," says author Zoë Heller. "Most of the time we spend painting the windows and doing the washing up to avoid it. But every now and then I'll read something that's so good — Saul Bellow, Martin Amis, Nadine Gordimer, V. S. Pritchett — and instead of making me feel depressed, feeling that, 'Oh, my god, I can never be as good as that,' it actually galvanizes me in some way and makes me want to rush off and start tip-tapping at the computer."

Read everything that's good. Start with Pulitzer Prize winners and National Book Award winners, the Booker Prize and Whitbread winners. If you want to write children's books, read Newbery winners, too.

set your timer

Reading teaches you about voice. Here's a way to experience an author's voice. Pick a novel, short story, or narrative nonfiction book by a favorite author and type out the first page or two. What is his or her sentence structure and does it vary? Is there a detectable rhythm? Simple or complicated vocabulary?

After you've copied a page or two, put the text aside. Set the timer for fifteen minutes (or longer) and carry on with the writing. Notice how the author's voice has affected your own. If you've read the book before, don't feel you must tell the story the author was telling. Tell your own story. Go with it.

overcoming the obstacles

that black hole: tv

My telling television moment came one evening as my son, Travis, then four, was watching Nickelodeon. When a sweet kids' show was interrupted by a trailer for an explosion-ridden movie that was more R-rated than G (or even PG), my displeasure was apparent. I whined and complained—not for the first time—about how one day I was going to get rid of cable. Travis must have been sick of my hands shielding his eyes, too, because one evening he said, "Get it cut off, Mom."

The next day I called up Comcast.

"Oh, did you get a satellite dish?" the cable representative asked.

"Uh, no," I said.

"No satellite?"

"We're just tired of cable," I said.

"You know, we always find out about illegal cable connections," he said, reminding me of my eighth-grade science teacher.

I'm so happy for you, I wanted to say.

That was five years ago. We haven't welcomed cable back into our home since. We use rabbit ears on the top of the TV when my son wants to watch Saturday morning cartoons or sports or on the extremely rare occasions when I watch PBS or the news. Once in a while Brian and I watch videos. Mostly, we just keep it turned off.

Television is one of the biggest time eaters on the planet. You don't realize how much time it steals from your life until you try to write or pursue another creative or personal venture. When you begin to live a writing life, you need to spend all spare moments writing to get momentum going.

Early on in my classes, I ask my new students how their week went and especially if they found time to get any writing done. Always I hear moaning or see scowls and then someone says she just couldn't find the time, she was so very busy. (It's usually a she; men in my classes hardly ever admit they sit in front of the tube unless it's to watch the news—that, they believe, is mandatory.) This is when I begin to lovingly berate her. I say, "Did you brush your teeth today?"

She nods.

"Did you get dressed?"

She nods, beginning to look guilty.

"Eat lunch? Dinner?"

She nods, seriously guilty.

"Make your bed?"

She's afraid to keep nodding, but her eyes say yes.

"Watch TV?"

She rolls her head, looks away, tries to keep from smiling. Caught!

Then the rationales begin: She only watches educational shows, *good* shows, like *Biography* or the nature shows (with her kids) and the home and cooking shows, just to relax.

"But it's all TV," I say. The good, fun, intelligent shows still eat up your time and you're pretty much left with nothing but less time in

which to write. If I had cable, I'd get sucked right in, too. "If you must watch," I admonish her and the rest who are guilty, "at least write first."

Other than taking up your time, watching too much TV has another downside. It can influence your writing in unsavory ways.

During the late eighties I watched soaps. So much so that if I was out when *All My Children* came on, I taped it. During this time I wrote a screenplay called *Corky & Annette*. An acquaintance read it and said, "Reads kind of like a soap opera." He didn't mean to make me feel bad, but I was crestfallen. Writing for the soaps was not my intent. At that very moment I knew it was time to stop watching them. I went cold turkey. That was how I quit smoking, too: I tamped it out and never lit up again. Now, when I walk into somebody's house where a soap is on the box, I feel a little sick to my stomach, the way I do when I'm among second-hand smoke.

Jennifer Lawler says, "When I was married, my husband and I had gotten into this terrible habit of watching television every night. It was better than actually communicating, since that always ended up in fights. When we divorced, I felt panicky, afraid I wouldn't be able to make a living as a freelancer. A friend who was helping me to move hauled my TV over to my new house, and as I sat there looking at it, all I could think was it would be a great way to ensure I never succeeded. So I sent the TV home with her. I've been TV-free for three years and haven't missed it at all. My daughter has no clue that other kids sit in front of the screen mesmerized—she's too busy playing. And I have an enormously successful freelance career with enough time left over to homeschool my daughter, spend time with my family and friends, and pursue my favorite hobbies."

I'm not suggesting that you stop watching all TV, just that you learn to restrict your watching (if you need help cutting down, read Jerry Mander's *The Four Arguments for the Elimination of Television*) and that you write before you let yourself turn it on. That way, when you think back to what you accomplished during the day, you will remember the writing—and reading—you did and not what happened to the characters on your favorite TV show.

Say you do get a lot of writing done during the day. What's wrong with staring bleary-eyed at the TV at night?

Freelance writer Beth Levine says, "We don't watch TV at all during the day. That's work time. At night, I got into the habit of falling in front of the TV after dinner, figuring I was way too played out to write anything. But I find that I do need to cut back on TV time at night for *think* time—to read, to process, to calm the noise in my brain, which is all necessary to the act of writing. You can't write if you don't have anything to say."

About the only way you will convince me that you need to watch *some* TV is if you're interested in *writing* for TV. Then you watch and study the form. (This will only work for so long; eventually you'll have to turn it off and start writing.)

Philip Reed, magazine editor, mystery author, and former TV writer, says, "TV writers are like idea machines, always ready with a new idea if the producer vetoes the last one. But I don't recommend watching a lot of TV if you want to write fiction. I've seen so many good ideas trashed by television, superficially explored and cheapened. Besides, sometimes knowing too much can be a problem. After a while, you begin to feel like every possible situation has already been used. I find this debilitating and counterproductive to writing. But then, I don't actually read a lot of mysteries, either, and for the same reason."

Foster the ability to say no: Reach for the remote, click off the box, then turn your hand to other things.

set your timer

For a week, keep a little notebook beside the TV and note every time you watch it. Write down the name of the show and how long you sat there. At the end of the week, assess your situation.

How much time are you spending? Have you had enough time to get the writing done that you wanted to do?

Now, set your VCR to tape your favorite show. Watch the first half of the show and then turn it off (but keep taping) and write the second half of the show. Or create a new character for the show. Watch the tape and see what the writers did. Unless, of course, you get too caught up in writing and forget.

*If your house is really a mess and a
stranger comes to your door, greet him with, "Who
could have done this? We have no enemies."*
—Phyllis Diller

housework

When I sit down to write, few things are as distracting as a messy house. (Well, there *is* e-mail . . .) Shoes and toys scattered about the floor, dirty dishes in the sink, slipcovers in disarray, and general clutter make it hard to concentrate on writing. I must first pick things up and put them away. And after I have, so much creative energy has been used up.

I'm hardly what you would call obsessive-compulsive about order. For instance, right now as I work, my son's plastic swords lie on the coffee table, Brian's huge vintage amplifier sits in the corner by the fireplace, and on the table close by are two three-pound dumbbells, two binders, a candle, eyeglasses, books and magazines, an antique china cup half filled with strong coffee doused with milk, and a well-worn ASJA membership directory. Draped over the back of the chair beside me is my orange-red silk robe that I bought in New York City's Chinatown a couple of years ago.

One might argue that with my immediate surroundings so

cluttered, how can I possibly work? To that I would say, it's *organized* clutter and every single thing nearby has a purpose. (The amp and miscellaneous stuff on the coffee table could go, and it will go, but right now it's so minimal it doesn't bother me.) And the items nearby have a certain aesthetic value to *me*; balled-up paper, dirty dishes, or yesterday's socks littering the floor are not the same.

"Clutter is the biggest obstacle to good energy," says author Mary Mihaly, a certified feng shui practitioner, "and when you really need to concentrate, clutter is a terrible distraction. For writers, who deal in paper, the mess can be overwhelming sometimes: Can I throw away this batch of notes? Will I need them again? Writers will notice the new energy, new productivity, if they clean out even one corner of an office and create new space for energy flow. Practicing good feng shui brings everything into your life that you need—including fresh information."

Christine Adamec, author of *Moms with ADD: A Self-Help Manual*, says, "One way you can get all the junk out of your office is to get new carpet. The carpet in my family room, where my office is, looked pretty bad. But to get new carpet, I had to clean up the piles of books and papers everywhere and ended up throwing out lots of stuff. For a while, it looked pretty good. Now the books and piles of papers are starting to pile up again."

If clutter gets to you and you use it as a reason not to write, here are a couple of solutions. The first is, if you like to work in the morning, deal with cleaning and getting your house or work space in order before you go to bed so that when you get up, you can turn your fresh energy to writing.

Another is to hire someone to help clean your house. When Brian and I became too busy with work and the house was in shambles and we had extra money, we hired Cornelia. She came once a week and took care of major things: changing the beds, cleaning the bathroom, dusting, vacuuming, and mopping the floors. I don't mind everyday cleaning—I even find it therapeutic—but the cleaning Cornelia did helped me have an entire day of writing. But when it came time to buy a new car, we went back to cleaning the house ourselves and used the money to put toward the monthly car payments. Plus, cleaning your own house can be gratifying. Sometimes I actually view cleaning as creating a giant work of conceptual art. And I know it's helping Travis learn good life skills.

Both clutter and cleaning can drain your energy and interfere with your writing. Only you can find the right balance—whether it's a change of routine or a change of attitude—that will leave you a space that is comfortable and allows time for the important things: your family, fun, and your writing.

set your timer

When you feel the urge to indulge in the immediately gratifying act of whitening the grout in your kitchen counter, sit down, set the timer, and write about a woman obsessed with cleaning. Take it to the extreme. Make her someone who drives people away because she's so determined to have a clean house that no one can truly relax there.

If you have someone cleaning your house, write about that person. What is her life like?

Write about items used for cleaning: vacuum cleaners, feather dusters, brooms, bleach, Windex. What images do these things conjure up? What memories do you associate with them? What was your house like growing up? What were your parents' attitudes about the house's appearance?

If you hate cleaning but feel your space weighing upon you, take that to the extreme, too. Create a fictional character who shares your sentiments and come up with an unusual solution or resolution. Or write an essay defending your offbeat view regarding housework.

See...you can use cleaning or clutter to your advantage without even getting up out of your chair.

Sweet are the uses of adversity.
—William Shakespeare

eddiction.com

T he problem with the Internet is not all the porn and spam and magic potion peddlers. Not for writers, anyway. The real problem is e-mail.

I am not alone in my addiction to e-mail. We e-mail addicts check our e-mail often throughout the day, although we try to resist the urge. About the only thing that helps me is going on vacation. When I'm out of town I feel like an idiot spending time online. There are too many other things to do.

E-mailing and surfing the Web can seem like work, but the truth is, unless you're actually doing research, you're not working. And even research can become an escape. Yes, you are writing when you e-mail, and this is good, but it is still not working. A 12-step group for e-mail addiction may be right around the corner.

Psychotherapist Dennis Palumbo believes—and you and I *know*—that constantly checking e-mail is one way writers procrastinate. "From a practical standpoint, e-mail is death to writers; the Internet *itself* is death to writers. I have a number of writer patients who have been so addicted to checking their e-mail once an hour or cruising the net that they've rented office space without phone jacks. If their wife or husband or child needs to reach them, they can use the cell phone. But they cannot get online."

Author Allison Johnson says, "If I'm really into a piece, I check e-mail later. I can turn off the noise blip that alerts [me] when one has come in. When I get in the zone, the flow, or whatever you call it, I don't want to be interrupted and will let the phone ring, etc. I won't eat or get up until I'm done. If you're easily distracted, you can also turn off the ringer and sound on the phone. People who have a hard time concentrating should take serious steps to minimize potential distractions."

Work on a computer that isn't e-mail ready so if you want to e-mail, you'll have to go to another computer that's connected to the Internet. Or, instead of going online each time you think of e-mail you must send, open your e-mail program, write the e-mail, and save it to send later. Or you can leave the house to work, taking your laptop or just a notebook. That's one way I've found to avoid checking e-mail; I take my laptop and go down the street to Café Zinc. Other writers leave the house to write, too. Crime writer Laura Lippman, who writes at a neighborhood café several days a week, says, "There's no phone at the coffeehouse, there's no e-mail. It has kind of that nice murmur that I remember from newsrooms, so I feel very much at home, sitting at a place where other people are talking, where phones ring, but no one is asking for my attention. It's a place where I can just focus, utterly, and I do. I still go down there almost every day. Most of my procrastination tools are not available to me when I'm there."

Keep foremost in your mind how much you want to get writing done. Reread an earlier chapter, "Stolen Moments," and learn to feel guilty if you don't write. (Here's one time guilt pays.) That may be the ultimate key: If you like yourself better when you write than when you don't, and if you don't like disliking yourself, then you'll make sure you get writing done before you spend time e-mailing.

Or you can use the e-mail distraction to your advantage. One morning after I walked my son to school, I came home and sat at my laptop. I didn't know where to begin, which chapter to work on. My mind was in a fog. So I did what most writers do at this point: I checked my e-mail.

There was a message from Jess, a student who has become a good friend. She talked about her writing and then she asked a simple question: *What's up with your book?*

The floodgates opened. But instead of talking about my book, I wrote nonstop about my newish neighbor, who was at that moment using her electric leaf blower to whisk the dust and debris from her patio. (What happened to *brooms*?) These neighbors have lived across the street for three months and we have barely smiled at one another. They use an outdoor heater when their friends are over. We live in a beach town. Who needs an outdoor heater on summer nights? This gives Californians a bad name. . . . In the midst of this vitriolic downpour, I stopped and noticed what I was doing. This was about more than my neighbors: *Take it a bit deeper, Babs. What's going on here?*

I missed A. J. and Sue, that's what it was. Their bungalow was torn down two years ago after they both died to make room for the monstrosity that obstructs the sky, where my new neighbors now live. I miss *all* the old people and their houses, which keep being torn down. History is being obliterated. I miss my parents who were old when they died.

I tell Jess all this and press SEND. Then I realize that when I want to get started and don't know where to begin, writing an e-mail to someone close to me works as a prompt. Because after I wrote to Jess, I started in on my book; I was sufficiently warmed up.

Going beyond the surface, reaching into the satchel of your own pet peeves and weaknesses and dark side, is not only good therapy and costs nothing, it can help you see how to flesh out your own fictional characters. Likewise, if you're writing a nonfiction piece—an essay, say—your understanding of weaknesses might help you to better understand the less-than-perfect nature of the people you're writing about.

Writing to one person, even if you have no intention of ever sending the e-mail or letter, can set your pen on fire and free up the feelings festering inside.

set your timer

Take fifteen minutes to respond to an e-mail correspondent you're especially close to or feel comfortable being verbose with. Begin with where you are. Go as deep as you can; deeper is where those verdant images and ideas and revelations reside.

Tell your friend how you are doing in as much detail as possible. If she asks what you did last night, tell her, right down to what you wore and what was said. Paint a picture of your night. If she asks how your kids are doing, go on and on, but be specific. Include dialogue and rich descriptions.

You don't need to send the reply if you don't want to. You actually may end up writing a short story or an essay or a vignette that you use in another work in progress.

I have contracted to write a book about
Vermont, and so find myself obsessed with Indiana.
—David Mamet

fickle minds

I t is a quirk of human nature to want what we don't have. I once had a boyfriend who liked me best when he wasn't so sure I liked him. When I'd break up with him, he'd fall for me all over again. When I gave in, when he had me and only me, he no longer was so sure I was what he wanted.

So it is with a writer's mind. When you have fifteen minutes to a half hour to write, it can be fairly easy working up to a fevered pitch because you want to use the little time you have. But say you have an entire afternoon or day splayed out in front of you, what then?

Or you get a book contract and a veritable compendium of choices present themselves: *I could work on my book, or I could bring out that short story I wrote last spring and what about that food novel I wrote and never sold?*

Ideas run amok. This is a good thing, especially when what you need are ideas. But when you already have an idea that you're committed to working on, you need to stay with it. When you get married, just because another handsome face or brilliant mind comes along doesn't mean you jump ship and set up house(boat) somewhere else, right?

It's so hard to keep this commitment. When writers have ideas, we want to pursue them.

I asked my friend, novelist Diane Leslie, if she ever feels fickle toward her writing projects.

"While I'm at the beginning of one book or story or play, I'm always fantasizing about writing something else or thinking I should write something else because no one will want to read what I am writing," she says. "But after I'm really into, say, a book, I get pretty involved and determined. I was always a better long-distance swimmer than a sprinter so I guess I have perseverance."

Ron Carlson says, "It's one thing to be writing a novel and take a week and write a story. But usually what you're doing is skating away from what's tough. Writing is tough. Staying in the room every day—please! You've got to be hardheaded about it. That's what I am: I'm hardheaded. I don't want the current story I'm working on to get away.

"You can write on the new idea—that's what I love about computers, open a file and go—but if you start that as a custom, you're going to end up with forty great, shining unfinished projects. Everybody I know is writing real good two-, three-, four-page stories, but then the fifth page gets tough and there it is. That's why desks have drawers. I'm interested in having the thing made. That's the difference between bright talented people and writers who are sometimes bright, sometimes talented, but real stubborn."

Dennis Palumbo says, "A lot of people experience a deadline as feeling exactly the same as handing in a paper in eighth grade: A powerful authority figure is going to grade what I do. The other part is when we have a deadline, we're very caught up in all of our stuff about performance and our insecurity about how we'll be seen or our concerns about whether we'll be employed again, or will we disappoint others. Well, compared to that range of feelings, who wouldn't want to turn to a project that interests them, and say, 'This is so interesting and fun, I bet my creativity will just flow.'"

Setting guidelines helps. When my agent sold this book, at first I felt totally inspired. It was all I wanted to work on. But as time went on, I started working on fiction again. Entire days would go by when I worked on fiction but not on this book. The trouble was, my contract was for this book, not for my novel.

So I made a deal with myself.

I could work on fiction, but only after I worked on this book. Fortunately, the point came, again, when this manuscript was all I thought about, and I didn't feel drawn to work on fiction at all. This is what I wanted to write and I wanted to make it as compelling as possible.

There's a certain heady feeling you get when you push through the desire to wander and focus in on one project to its satisfying end.

set your timer

If you have more than one project going, or more than one idea bobbing about your brain, which one do you want to work on over all others? Which do you find yourself thinking about, musing over? Choose one, put the others away, and focus on the one you've chosen.

Give yourself a deadline and treat it seriously. Even on days when your interest level is flagging, work on your project for just fifteen minutes. See it to its conclusion.

When your mind is pulled in the direction of another project, pull it back. Understand that the impulse to wander is like a wild pony that has to be corralled. Be careful not to mistake being fickle for being bored.

When you get in a tight place and everything goes against you
till it seems as though you could not hold on a minute longer, never give
up then, for that is just the time and the place the tide will turn.
—Harriet Beecher Stowe

rejection

Medical students serve internships. So do lawyers and veterinarians. Even hairdressers and masseuses put in many required hours before they receive their licenses.

Yet writers entertain the myth that they don't need to serve an internship. In their first writing class, if they don't produce a publishable story, or at least one that everyone considers marvelous, some feel they must be one of the most dull, untalented beings this side of Jupiter. A year later, if they still haven't sold anything—a common scenario—their fixation worsens.

We all want it so quickly. Where is our patience?

One day at the end of a class, after everyone else had left, Tanya, a student in her midtwenties with a degree in writing but no publication credits thus far, approached me. Puffing on a cigarette, she wanted to know what I really thought: Did she have any talent? Should she continue writing? Her pain and insecurity were palpable, and I wanted to soothe her however I could.

I recited the litany I knew by heart because I had said it so often: If she were in a degree program in college or graduate school, and not in a private writing workshop, she would not even consider starting her publishing career yet.

While some writers like Truman Capote, Michael Chabon, and Ann Beattie seem to hit the ground running and find success early, most writers don't. I told Tanya what someone once told me: You must write hundreds of thousands of words before any of them stick. I mentioned William Kennedy, who was stone-broke and fifty-something before he published *Ironweed*, gained recognition, and went on to win the Pulitzer Prize in 1984. Jo-Ann Mapson claims her first book was so awful she can't stand to look at it and is amazed that Boston University even wanted to collect it with her papers. Jonathan Kellerman has something like eight unpublished novels under his bed, and his wife, Faye Kellerman, has four.

Elizabeth George wrote three novels without getting published. Finally, she published her "first" novel, *A Great Deliverance*, and won an Agatha and an Anthony Award, major honors in the mystery world. "The thing that sustained me," says George, author of more than a dozen novels, "was a quote I cut out from the *Los Angeles Times* that said the people who get published are the people who never give up. P. D. James said the same thing to me, four years before my first novel came out. 'My dear,' she said, 'you've done something that most people only dream of, you've written a novel. You must never give up.'"

It's that effort over time that counts. "So much of this is apprenticeship, craft, and experience," says Betsy Lerner, literary agent and author of *The Forest for the Trees*. "Many of the first novels that we read are really somebody's fifth novel. I never want to tell a person, 'Try ten times and quit,' because we all know of the stories where it was the twenty-first submission that got them in."

And determination is ultimately as crucial as sheer talent. As best-selling celebrity biographer and journalist Pat Broeske said when she came on my show, "I'm not the most talented writer around, but I show up for the job."

In a beginning creative writing class that I teach at UCI, Kathryn Atkins, a student who had returned to school in midlife, asked if I knew writers who weren't so great at the beginning who went on to publish. The look on her face told me she worried my answer would be no.

I said I have seen the most mediocre writers go on to publish essays, short stories, travel articles, nonfiction books, and novels, and I've seen some of the most talented writers do nothing at all.

These talented people typically start sending their stuff out and, like all writers, get rejected—because all writers, at every stage, get rejected—and they soon give up. They may not quit writing, but they quit taking it seriously. They get good jobs, advanced degrees, open businesses, surmount obstacles, but they can't deal with being turned down by editors.

I added that it's better to get rejected than be published before your work is ready and be subjected to awful reviews that could destroy your writing career when it has barely gotten going.

Rejection is a part of the writing life. The sooner you come to terms with it, the better. Yes, a lucky few start writing, send their work to an agent, and a year later their first book is out. More common, though, are the writers who persevere for months, even years, before ever seeing anything resembling success. They figure if they're getting rejection letters, at least they're in the game and it's only a matter of time.

Tom Paine, author of *The Pearl of Kuwait*, says his short stories were rejected for ten years. He tried quitting, wrote advertising copy, became a journalist. But he kept coming back to fiction and finally started getting published—in the *New Yorker*, no less.

Many famous bestsellers were rejected many times: *Zen and the Art of Motorcycle Maintenance, Ironweed, The Diary of Anne Frank, Carrie, Animal Farm, Lolita.* Check out André Bernard's *Rotten Rejections* and you'll feel better when you see how many now-famous authors had a hard time.

Judith Ryan Hendricks was shocked when her first novel, *Bread Alone*, sold to HarperCollins and then to publishers in other countries. "The way it happened was a fairy tale. I got my share of rejections from agents, and when it happened, it happened suddenly. I took a class with Jo-Ann Mapson, she liked the manuscript, sent it to her agent, Deborah Schneider, and two weeks later I had an agent, after almost a year of sending it out and getting postcards back saying, 'I don't have time to read this' or 'We're not taking on new authors' or 'This is not our kind of book.' Those I didn't take personally. Some were very unpleasant. There's no need for that. They would write sarcastic comments, even on my cover letter, and send it back to me, which I thought was a bit much. And some were very, very nice, and tried to be helpful. One lady wrote me a single-spaced letter of advice about how to get published and said, 'I wish I could help you, but I'm getting out of the business and moving to Mexico'!"

Sometimes rejection is just a matter of taste: What one agent or editor passes on, another will love. But you can also learn from rejection how you might revise your work to make it salable. Often some small aspect of the presentation, the angle or the like, needs to change. You've just got to be committed to your project. If you are, you will withstand rejection and ultimately triumph. Every piece of writing I've been committed to has made it through all the nos to find a yes.

"Every rejection that comes is very personal," says Mary Yukari Waters, author of *The Laws of Evening*, "and you think, oh, I'm not good, and then later you look at the story and you can see why they rejected it. It's partly talent and technique, surely, but if all that is decent, it becomes about personal taste. Certain people are drawn to certain sensibilities, certain topics. It's like going to a party: You don't expect every single person to like you, but maybe one or two will. That's what you're going for. One of my stories in the Pushcart Prize received more than three dozen rejections and I kept sending it out because I felt it should be published and [I] finally placed it in *Shenandoah*. Also, you assume you'll have an easier time with the less prestigious magazines, but I've found that that's not the case at all. I've had several stories taken by very good magazines that were rejected by the lower tiers."

Betsy Lerner says, "It can be difficult to handle rejections. But I sometimes tell people there are two responses: yes and no. You've got to keep trying to find that person who loves it, if you're one of those people with the stamina to send it out twenty times. Or you put it aside and move to the next work, which will undoubtedly be better than the work you just completed."

Good work eventually finds publication — but not by itself. You need to work at that, too. In the mid-eighties, one of my goals was to write travel articles. I loved reading about travel, so, on my third trip to Rajasthan, India, I went equipped with a good camera and a notebook.

On my third day there, as the day edged toward sunset, a few of us made our way to Baba's rock, an outcropping of boulders that overlooks a vast plain bordering Pakistan. I was in a bad mood — jet lag, still? — so I got out my Nikon and began snapping away, running through rolls of slide film. Getting creative usually helps me overcome negativity's pull.

A group of white-saried female Brahma Kumari yogis with long braids hanging down their backs joined us. When the sunset reached a beguiling shade of periwinkle, the women and my companions situated themselves on the rocks to watch. I continued to photograph. My bad mood lifted. I felt transported. I knew I was on to something. When the sun reached the middle of the sky, it disappeared, as if through a buttonhole. But not before I shot more than one hundred exposures and forgot all about my gray mood.

Three weeks later, back in San Francisco, I planned a travel article on India. I love India, and I love travel writing. I'd never written a travel piece before, and I wanted to — but how to begin?

I signed up for a class and some months later completed the course and my article. (Since then, I've learned to query first, and *then* write the article.) I was passionate about Mount Abu and figured there had to be an editor out there who would feel the same.

I wrote to in-flight and travel magazines and gathered a file of rejection letters. It was time to get creative. Korean Airlines' in-flight magazine, *Morning Calm*, wasn't listed in any of the writers resource books, so I called the airline's advertising office in Los Angeles. They suggested sending the department a letter describing the project.

A month later I received a reply in a blue onionskin airmail envelope from Seoul: "We are very interested in your idea," Mr. Kim said, "and we are interested in the mountain itself. Please send us your article and tell us what sort of remuneration you would like."

The mountain itself? And they wanted *me* to tell *them* what *I* wanted to be paid?

I wrote another letter detailing the pay range of other in-flights and enclosed the article and copies of the slides. Several months later I received a check for close to $900. Later, I resold the piece to other markets and totaled $1,400 for that one piece. It was the most money I've ever made for one travel article.

Seeing that article in print, with the photo of the yogis watching the sunset, and other photos filled me with a sense of accomplishment and the realization that when you believe in something you're working on, despite the challenge of writing and marketing and dealing with rejection, you have to keep at it until it gets published or you lose interest.

So many talented writers give up. The rejection process is too painful, and publication takes too long. And writers have a habit of becoming so discouraged after sending out their work and being rejected that they put writing aside for lucrative and useful careers as real estate agents, teachers, and therapists.

You must ask yourself why you write, and while your reasons may include to publish a book or get back at an old boyfriend who believed he was a better writer, the writing itself must be the first thing.

Find the part of you that is an eternal optimist, the part that says, "Why *not* me?" Have that part of you market your work and don't take no for an answer.

set your timer

If rejection scares you, can you figure out what it is about rejection that's scary? What is the worst that can happen? Take a little time and free-associate, starting with the word *rejection*. Write down everything you think of, however tangential. Wend your way around the word, get to know it.

Then think of a time when you were rejected either in writing or in another way. Set your timer and write about this — in a first-person essay or create a character, based on you, and tell how she was rejected. Was it by a boyfriend in high school or an employer at a job? By a parent or a sibling or an aunt?

Rejection, for a writer, ultimately means you are closer to being published. You've produced work and sent it out. No one does this by accident, so perhaps it's time to consider your plans. What are they? Write down your goals for the next month, six months, year, five years. Allow your fantasies to range far and wide. Be outrageous! What's your dream? Be as specific as possible. Detail the types of writing you want to do and where you would love to be published.

When writing becomes difficult or you find yourself confronting rejection, remember those goals. If you allow fear to overtake you, an editor or publisher will never have the option of publishing your work. You might end up becoming one of those "should have, would have, could have" people. And to my way of thinking, few things could be worse. Committing to your writing goals gives you a fighting chance.

Envy is one of the scorpions of the mind,
often having little to do with the objective, external world.
—Bonnie Friedman, WRITING PAST DARK

green with envy

I t begins early in life. Other kids have the best games, the best
dolls, the best houses. Since he's been in the first grade, Travis
occasionally says, "So and so is so lucky, he..." Fill in the blank: has
a Nintendo, a PlayStation, a big backyard, or is going to Ruby's for
lunch. His friends do the same: Other kids are luckier than they are.

As you grow older, envying toys is replaced with envying someone
else's job, body, talents, or success. Envy is normal; everyone has moments of it. But unless we take control, envy can wreak havoc on our
lives and destroy any pleasure we get from creativity.

And we women can be *so* insecure. We're never pretty enough,
thin enough, or smart enough. Any smidgen of talent we possess
we're sure is a fluke. A writer tends to be more reflective than the typ-
ical person; we magnify our faults. And we're not only jealous of our
own shadow, but those of other women and men, too.

Psychotherapist Dennis Palumbo says, "The only difference between men and women that I've seen, regarding how envy manifests,

is that, due to social conditioning, men tend (and this is a *gross* generalization) to express — or even experience — their envy as an anger or dismissal of the one being envied. Usually, this anger is a cover for feelings of shame and inadequacy.

"On the other hand, women artists feel shame for *having* the envy, seeing it either as an indication of low self-worth or confirmation that they're not talented enough. In other words, women seem to be in competition with other women; men seem to be in competition with some high-achievement self-ideal, instilled in them in childhood, before which they always fall short."

I recently experienced this. One group of creative writing students — adults from their twenties to seventy — asked to read my first published short story. I suppose they wanted a window into my past, wanted to see who I was and what sort of work I was doing when I first began writing and publishing. I hesitated at first; the story was riddled with flaws; I'd write it differently now. Yet, I relented: It would be good for them to see that even the most imperfect story can make it to print in a decent literary journal. It might inspire them.

But reading my story caused an unexpected reaction in one of my students. Rather than becoming inspired, it sent Jess, a talented writer in her late twenties, into a tailspin. How did I ever write such a wonderful, nuanced story at such a young age? She worried she'd never be able to do the same.

From my point of view, her fear — and envy — had no real basis. Jess started writing seriously six months ago and has such natural talent and such heart, I'm sure if she continues, she will do incredible things. On the other hand, her temporary paralysis made perfect sense. After I received my B.A. and published my first short story, I stopped writing for a year, so busy was I comparing myself to accomplished authors.

Envy does have its positive side. It can be a great motivator. If we channel it appropriately, it can serve to propel us on, make us reach further than we might normally. So much of good writing comes from reading. As well as being inspired by books, we can be moved to create because we believe we could do just as well—or better—than another author did or because the work unlocks a part of us where there's a story that yearns to see print.

When he came on my show, Billy Collins gave voice to this: "Writing is a combination of reading and jealousy. There are some people who are lifetime readers and are just happy to take in the words of others. But writers are people who, at some point, read something that makes them furious with jealousy because they haven't written it. At that point they decide, at some level of consciousness, that they are going to write, too. I think the great muse is envy."

The next time envy plants itself beside you, look at what it wants to show you, then let it motivate you. Remember there isn't a writer alive who hasn't felt envy at one time or another, even those authors you consider the best and the brightest. Virginia Woolf and other authors you hope to emulate had their demons. Woolf often *hated* her own work. Once you accept that all writers have felt this way, you'll learn to acknowledge your feelings and get back to work.

set your timer

There exists a fine line between admiration and envy. Who do you admire/envy? Does it undo you, stop you from writing, or does it spur you on?

Imagine being your own idol and having to live up to the reputation bestowed upon you by your fans, by the media. Dennis Palumbo relayed a story Norman Mailer once told about having writer's block because he was no longer just a guy trying to write, he was Norman Mailer, and had to live up to Norman Mailer's reputation.

Read a bit from your idol's work, absorbing the cadence, the way the words hit the page, tone and point of view. Then set the timer for fifteen minutes and write a piece as if you were your idol: Write about yourself, your own life, and how it is to be you. How do you, as your idol, feel about yourself? Do you feel enviable, or are you sunk in the muck like everyone else? Who do you envy? What would the idol you've chosen envy about your own life?

Fear is a sign — usually a
sign that I'm doing something right.
—Erica Jong

trusting fear

How is it possible to get work done when there's so much to worry about?

Some years back, when my son, Travis, was still in diapers and Brian and I were overprotective new parents, a magazine editor assigned me to do a travel piece, so Brian, Travis, and I drove out to spend three days at a Palm Springs resort. The November morning sun was bright and warm, and the sky was an unreal shade of blue. We ate breakfast on the patio of the hotel's restaurant.

"Why do you think he's not peeing?" I said to Brian as Travis played with a fork and a spoon.

"It's not even noon," said Brian.

"He hasn't peed in more than twelve hours!"

"He'll pee," said Brian.

"Are you wet, Trav?" I said.

"Not wet," said Travis.

"Drink your apple juice," I said.

"Don't worry," said Brian. "I never heard of a kid not peeing."

"I'm sure it's happened," I said.

"Why would he not pee?" Brian leaned back as the waiter refilled his coffee cup.

"Maybe the hole closed up," I said.

"Oh, God," said Brian.

"Let me check your diaper." I reached over to Travis.

"Not wet!" he said, but he was wet, finally, and the day shone brighter as a wave of optimism washed over me.

"We've been given a reprieve," I told Brian.

I no longer worry about my son's ability to pass water, but I do worry about other things: whether we'll ever buy a house, whether Brian will have a busy holiday season, whether today will be the day we have the Big One — that earthquake all Californians dread — and if we do, will termites make our rented bungalow fall down?

Brian says he has reasons to worry, Lord knows, but it doesn't occur to him. Brian's glass is three-quarters full. Mine, half empty.

What are the solutions? Drugs, exercise, a partial lobotomy, but with my luck, the surgeon would take the wrong side and I'd end up in the *National Enquirer* with the headline, WOMAN THINKS SHE'S IGUANA.

How do you write when there's so much to worry about? If you're a worrier, rather than fretting away the day or eating too much or calling your friends with your tales of woe, write. Writing helps diffuse worry, helps you become more rational and see worry for what it is.

Of course, there's worry and then there's fear. There are vague worries that haunt us, that accompany us throughout our day, with no real base in reality. Then there are times when things are downright bleak, whether because of money or health or other very real problems. It's truly hard, then, to muster the wherewithal to write.

You may be in a black mood because you just balanced your checkbook and only have one hundred dollars left to your name.

The bills on the kitchen counter are piled high and even though money may be on the way, it's not here yet, and your car needs tires or your child needs dental work or your best pair of shoes has a hole and you have a job interview tomorrow. Things may be going badly at work, your best friend may no longer be speaking to you, or you may have the sneaky suspicion your lover is seeing another honey.

Worst of all are health problems. When you're not feeling well or are dealing with a major health worry—yours or someone else's—it's nearly impossible to write. The mind needs to be in a relaxed state to be creative. How can you tap into that pool of creativity when your brain is jangled with what-ifs or doctors' appointments?

During tough times, I take support wherever I can find it—from writers, both living and dead, and from my faith. A writers group helps, too, especially if it contains at least a few writers struggling as you are. Writers who once struggled but are now successful (while you may secretly envy and despise them a little) can be touchstones: They offer hope and possibility, the knowledge that things can and do change.

Certain people begin writing because life is gloomy. "I started writing fiction in adulthood *because* things were bleak," says my student Candice Harper. "At a time when my life seemed completely out of my control, when I was dogged by anxiety and depression and didn't believe anyone could help me find a way out, I wrote. I wrote badly and prolifically, and I survived."

It helps to hear about writers who've written through desperate times. They give me hope that I can make it through things that may seem impossible at the time. Carolyn See is one example: She wrote *Making a Literary Life* as her partner of twenty-five years lay dying not far from her desk.

When her baby son was ill, Dani Shapiro found it impossible to write much at all. Fortunately, her memoir, *Slow Motion*, had just been bought by Sony/Phoenix Pictures and she and her screenwriter husband, Michael Maren, were hired to write it.

"That is probably the only project that I could have actually done while my son was sick," says Shapiro, "because I was working on it with a partner who was also going through the same thing I was going through. We would close ourselves off in a room together for a few hours a day and work. It was a godsend because I could have never been working on a novel then. I longed for a day job.

"When you're a writer, your head is where you live, and if your head is in a distracted or uncomfortable or painful place, that's all you've got."

There are times when it is just too damn hard to do any writing, let alone keep your life together. But have faith that you will still be a writer when they pass.

"There will always be periods in life when it just *isn't* possible to write, whether because of personal crisis or other important demands on our time," says author Taylor Smith. "But the muse doesn't go away. On the contrary, these periods of intense living can recharge the creative well, particularly if we live in the moment, conscious of all the nuances of joy, sorrow, and pain that life entails. When we eventually and inevitably get back to the writing, I think it's stronger and richer for our having fully lived."

Some writers draw on their strengths with what is difficult and scary. When she came on my show, Susan Straight, author of *Highwire Moon* and other novels, essays, and short stories, said fear inspires her to write fiction.

"I once called my agent and told him, 'What I'm writing is so scary I have a stomachache.'" She says that occasionally when she's writing—which tends to be late at night after her daughters are in bed—she becomes so afraid by what she's written that she has to leave the computer and walk about the house. My kids will come out from their rooms, worried someone's breaking in. 'No, no,' I tell them, 'I'm just working on a scary part of the book.' I can imagine what they tell their friends at school."

Jacquelyn Mitchard goes further than most of us are willing to venture; in her books, kids are lost, people die. Her first novel, *The Deep End of the Ocean,* was about a child who disappears in a department store and isn't found for twelve years. Her latest book is about a woman who, on her fourteenth wedding anniversary while out to dinner with her husband, gets a crushing headache and soon learns she has a brain aneurysm and will die in twenty-four hours. I asked Mitchard how she was able to write such deeply emotional books about topics that *could* happen.

"It's very scary," she said. "Today I had a bad headache, and I thought, Oh, no!... I often write about things that are terribly draining to write about and it's almost like after having done it, after having spent time with the characters in the book, it's like having swum a very long way and climbing up on the beach wet and exhausted."

Facing that which is difficult to consider can be a blessing for a writer. Do you fear what apparently many women fear (according to a not-so-recent survey): aging and either going crazy or becoming homeless, or both? Are you afraid of something happening to your child, your partner? Do you worry that one day you or someone you adore will be on an airplane along with some crazy guy wielding, if not a box cutter, some other dangerous instrument?

Writing about your fears won't make them come true. It may not even dispel them. What it will do is allow you to write about something that moves you that you have invested energy in.

Years ago I read Frank Herbert's science fiction novel *Dune* and loved it for its wisdom regarding fear. I wrote an excerpt on a three-by-five card and kept it for years on or in my desk:

Fear is the mind-killer. Fear is the little death that brings total obliteration. I will face my fear. I will permit it to pass over me and through me. And when it has gone past, I will turn the inner eye to see its path. Where the fear has gone there will be nothing. Only I will remain.

That quote so applies to writers and writing. That's exactly how it is to go into and through the fear and become stronger for it. If you let fear stop you, you will never get any writing done.

set your timer

I want you to make two lists: One list is your worries, another is what makes you happy. Now create two characters and pour your worries into the worrier and give the other all your optimism, pleasure, and hope—all those things that make you happy.

Put the two characters together—at a party, at a restaurant, at a quilting bee—and have them interact. What happens? What do they say to each other? What conflict arises? Writers often find that they learn something when they live vicariously through their characters, at least for a while, and our best characters always have something to teach us. Students tend to like this exercise because it deals in contrasts. My student Liz Morgan says, "The interesting thing for me was to find that there was so much overlap, each experiencing joy and melancholy simultaneously. The characters never became one-dimensional for me, even when I was focusing on those specific characteristics."

If you prefer writing essays, address this topic in that form. Write about worry itself or research a topic that's worrying you and write an article.

What about what you're afraid of? Does anything cause you to wake in the middle of the night in a cold sweat? What gives you nightmares? What is it exactly that you are afraid of?

Pick one of these fears and give it form. Either write a 500-word essay about something you dwell on, or use the fear as a theme for a short story. Fears can also be a source of humor: Think Woody Allen.

Play with your fear. For instance, if you're worried about fires, create a character that lives in a fire zone, who can't get fire insurance and lives there anyway, and one day has to deal with life-threatening fire. What does she do? Is she victorious? Does she save her home and the neighborhood? Does she lose her house and later, sifting through the ashes, come across her long-dead mother's wedding ring?

Use every morsel of your experience — actions, thoughts, fears, hopes, dreams, obsessions — and you will never ever, as long as you live, run out of material.

There are two ways of spreading light:
to be the candle or the mirror that reflects it.
—Edith Wharton

mentors

You're going along, liking what you're working on, so you bring it to your writers group. For the most part, everyone likes it, but you focus on the negatives, the things people say aren't working so well. Or they tear it apart, and you go home troubled, sure you will never be a writer. The next morning you feel haunted by the ghosts of self-doubt. Maybe you really should forget about this writing stuff. Thank god you didn't quit your day job. And what made you think you could work and write at the same time, anyway?

This is the time it helps to have a mentor. Mentors have pulled me through many tough times.

During the summer between my second and third year of college, I lived in the hills of West Virginia. I hauled water from a well and split wood to cook with. I sold jewelry I made at crafts fairs. Returning to school to continue pursuing a B.A. in liberal arts, majoring in photography, made less and less sense to me. Here

I was living off the land, doing something useful, practical, life sustaining.

When I returned to Goddard College in the fall—to quit, presumably—I sought out Jeff Weiss, my photography teacher and mentor. We stood in his gravel driveway across from a beaver pond.

"You want to go back to West Virginia and do *what?*" he said. "Be an earth mother? That's what you're going to do with your life, be an *earth mother?*" He scratched at his dark beard. "C'mon, what do you *really* want to do?"

I gazed across the street at the dam that beavers had constructed in his pond. Branch by branch they built it, no matter how often Jeff said he tore it down. I loved writing, but it seemed so impossible to construct a life around it. Didn't you have to be brilliant and have a huge vocabulary to write?

I finally whispered, "I've always wanted to write." I could hardly believe I was admitting to this.

"So, write!" he said. "Take a class with Judith. She's getting published. It's a hard life, but hell, if that's what you want, go for it."

Judith Beth Cohen was his wife, a real live writer with publication credits. She became my first writing mentor and made me believe I could become a writer.

Another decisive moment occurred a year later, at the beginning of my fourth year of college. I wanted to spend a semester away from writing to focus on the performing arts. I had acted in some theater and some TV—and I thought I missed it. What was really going on was I had hit a rocky place in my writing and it was time to move to the next level. That's always the hardest part. At these times you want to quit.

My advisers wouldn't allow it. They ganged up on me. "You're a writer," they said. "You have to keep writing."

At first I was shocked. Later I felt gratified. They had supplied the confidence when I had none. I still think of them with gratitude;

they were mentors to me even before the word *mentor* was a part of my lexicon.

Mentors show up when you're ready. Noreen Ayres, a mystery writer, says her mentor was her first creative-writing teacher when she was twenty-five. "My writing teacher told me he read one of my stories to his night class. He said that when he read it, a young man had to get up and leave because it affected him so much, and I thought, well, I guess I can do that; I can write."

National Book Award winner Alice McDermott says she found her mentor when she was a sophomore in college. "I had a wonderful, *wonderful* writing teacher," she says. "He is the reason I continue teaching myself. He told me I was a writer. I didn't know it until he told me, and as soon as he told me, I realized I'd always known it. Although I made stabs at doing other things, I knew very quickly there wasn't much else I could do that would allow me to sleep well at night and wake up with any enthusiasm."

One of my students, Karen Wilson, says, "As I fall headlong into each abyss, my mentors remind me of their identical temptation to stray from fortitude. They show me through their own work exactly how they have succeeded. And I breathe relief because I am motivated to reopen the work and begin anew. Without these coaches, these truth-speakers, I would dye my hair, polish my nails, buy new shoes, and seek some other form of expression in this world—but not by writing it down."

Sure, you can probably do it without a mentor, but I've found that those who continue to move along the writing path and continue to progress are those who have mentors. Look for someone you trust who always has your writing welfare in mind, and you may have found your mentor. Mentors can be found in writing classes, the place most of us begin, or even at workshops and conferences. Wherever you find your mentor, find her. Few things are as valuable in life as being able to rely on a person you trust who cares deeply about your writing, your career, and you.

set your timer

Take fifteen minutes and call your local university extension or community college and see what writing classes are offered or go online and look for nearby classes. Visit a bookstore and talk to people who work there about writers groups they offer. Attend readings and get to know other writers. Call the group whose flyer you found at a coffeehouse. Go online to *Readerville.com* or *Poets & Writers* magazine's Speakeasy message forum (*www.pw.org*) to find a virtual writing community.

There's a saying from the Eastern wisdom traditions that when the student is ready, the teacher will appear. The teacher may be a single individual or a whole group of people. Some of us are lucky enough to be part of a community of writers who collectively mentor one another.

Prepare the ground. See yourself as a writer. If you're not published yet, don't despair. Writers write. Keep writing, look for support, and find a mentor. And when the words just won't come or when a form-letter rejection colors your entire day gray, someone will be there to remind you that you are a writer and to tell you to get back to work.

Talk uses up ideas... Once I have spoken them aloud, they
are lost to me, dissipated into the noisy air like smoke. Only if I
bury them, like bulbs, in the rich soil of silence do they grow.
—Doris Grumbach, FIFTY DAYS OF SOLITUDE

keep your lips sealed

When you have an idea for a story, essay, or book, it's such a great feeling. It's a little like falling in love. You want to talk about it, tell all your writer friends, go over each little detail, every nuance, your hopes and plans.

While it's fine to describe a new love, it is not fine to describe a new project. As you talk, that inspiration, *that charge*, dissipates. You let the air out of it. It's one thing to write and then read what you've written to your writers group; it's another thing to talk about it before you've written it.

"You got to be real careful about taking the lid off the pot, even with close friends, *even with your wife*," says writer Ron Carlson. "I keep guard until I have enough that I'm safe. It's so tempting, especially when you have a few good mornings in a row, and then you're in a group of people, you're having lunch. There's a little silence before coffee... But you better not. Just fold your hands, and when you're asked how it's going, you say, 'Well, I'm working, I worked this morning.' That's good. You don't have to say what happened."

Talking about your work and letting the air out is a danger, *especially* if you're a talker. Dennis Palumbo agrees. "I believe good writing is private. I used to feel that the more I talked about my writing and what I was doing specifically, the more the magic would go away. Its specialness would start to be diluted for me.

"Plus, from a practical standpoint, if you show unfinished work to people — fifty pages or something — even when they like it a lot, in my experience, they'll say something that makes you crazy. They'll go, 'And boy, I really love this character of the brother,' and you're thinking, But I'm going to kill my brother off in the next chapter, and your whole faith in the book goes away because this person is going to be unhappy that the brother died. It's dangerous to show people unfinished work. The only exception to what I just said is the buddy system. Every writer needs a buddy. More than a good editor, agent, or a therapist, a writer needs a buddy. That's that one person you *can* give unfinished work to or you *can* spitball your ideas with, [knowing that whatever] this person tells you, they're not going to derail you. They're going to try to make the thing you're doing work better on its own terms — not the way they would write it, but help you write it the way you want to write, and usually for writers if they — if *you* — find more than one of this kind of person, it's a miracle. Every writer needs one."

There's another exception: If you are at an impasse and you don't know what to do next, it may help to discuss your work with one person you trust who isn't necessarily a writer. I have at times brainstormed with my husband, writer friends, even my young son, and they have provided excellent solutions. When I do, I ask specific questions, focusing on a chapter or a character.

But when it comes to discussing your work in broad terms — don't do it. Keep your lips sealed.

set your timer

Take fifteen minutes and try planning a story. Write a paragraph to summarize what it will be about. Then, by writing for fifteen minutes a day for a week, try to complete a first draft of your story before you mention it to anyone. It may take all the strength you can muster not to talk about it. You'll feel that discomfort that comes when you're trying to overcome any bad habit. You may sweat a little, you may squirm. If you're a stress eater, you may eat more than usual (keep celery and carrots at the ready).

Keeping your lips sealed is all about willpower, and anything requiring that much willpower takes practice. The urge will be there, sometimes outrageously so, to blab about what you're working on. But if you can manage not to utter a word, your work will be better for it.

My two pieces of advice for writers are:
(1) Keep your overhead as low as possible and
(2) Never live with someone who
doesn't respect your work.
—Grace Paley

significant others

There are a number of writing couples who have enviable partnerships: Michael Chabon and Ayelet Waldman, Jane Shore and Howard Norman, my friends Tony Eprile and Judith Schwartz. Writers living together usually have a simpatico relationship. They understand each other's sensibility and respect each other's need for solitude.

But what about when your partner, for whatever reason, feels threatened? Deliberately or not, a partner like this can kill your creativity—or the relationship. A nonwriter doesn't necessarily understand how you can be there but not there. The two of you might be having a conversation, and you're imagining a scene you're working on that takes place in a villa in Sicily, thinking about what you can do to fix it, or he's talking to you and you're trying to listen, you really *want* to listen, but what you truly want even more is for him to stop talking and leave you to your thoughts. You love him, but can't he see you're trying to work?

Or he casually glances at your notebook, or scenes you've typed out. After all, your materials just *happen* to be within reach; what's the harm? But what he reads he takes all wrong. Compound that with how he just invaded your privacy and you've got one combustible situation. This can be the undoing of a relationship, especially if it happens repeatedly. Or it can be the beginning of an understanding about what it's like to live with a writer.

During the first year or so that my husband and I lived together, Brian read an entry in my freewriting notebook. It just happened to be on the arm of the sofa. He walked by and accidentally knocked it to the floor. He said he couldn't help but notice a few words that piqued his curiosity, so he picked it up and read a page.

Now, in our house, there are tablets, notebooks, journals, and stray pieces of paper all over the place. I would never think of reading any that belonged to Brian, so I felt the hairs rise on the back of my neck, especially when he started quizzing—no, interrogating—me about the time I lived in San Francisco, and was that an ex-boyfriend, the Rastafarian, in that freewriting he "accidentally" saw?

I started explaining it was fiction and that I was doing what fiction writers do—drawing a little from here, a little from there, embellishing, fabricating—but as I explained, I grew angry. He had no right to look at my notebook, no matter if it did splay open at his feet. I told him this was one of those deal breakers; there was no way I could live in a house and not trust that my notebooks were private property, even if they were left out on the table or laying open on the floor. We did what couples do: We argued our sides. Luckily, we came to an understanding.

As a writer, you need to do two things: Set boundaries and then take it easy. Living with a writer can be hard to contend with. Understand your poor partner may be worried, whether he knows it or not, that his entire being—every personality glitch and flaw—might someday be exposed.

This comes up in most writers' relationships, usually early on. My student Phil Doran, former TV writer and author of the forthcoming *The Reluctant Tuscan*, says, "When Nancy and I were first living together, I was working on a TV show about a group of young women. I asked Nancy what they used to tease her about when she was in school. She told me that she used to have real skinny arms, so they called her 'chicken arms.' I instantly put that in a script and when Nancy saw the show she freaked out. I asked what she was all worked up about. 'I never said it was you!' I told her. From then on, she knew she was living with a psychic vampire and she had better be careful about anything she told me."

If you've had the experience of being written about, then you know. Recently I was the subject of an essay published by a friend in the Sunday magazine of a major newspaper. I had anxiety attacks prior to the piece coming out. This was a good friend and he'd told me what was in the essay, though I hadn't read it, and I trusted him — to a point. But not until I read the printed piece did I relax.

Living with a writer is stressful for Brian. He's a private man. When he fell in love with me, I doubt he fell in love with the idea of exposure. He didn't even think about it.

"The first time my personal life appeared in a magazine article written by you," Brian told me, "I was shocked and angry and not consoled a bit by the name changes. The man being discussed obviously was and would be recognized as me. It doesn't matter if it's fiction or nonfiction; it's what's revealed that can be upsetting.

"Chances are that a spouse who reads something previously kept secret from them will get upset. But I'm less shocked every time an article is published that contains something I'm unhappy about. It's like stepping into cold water; after a while you get used to it. At least I did. I think."

Significant others accidentally confuse their partner's personal life with their work. My friend and former student Allison Johnson said her husband, William, once picked up a short story she left on her desk. It was a quirky story about a ne'er-do-well pool boy/Casanova's relationships with lonely women. After reading the story, William went to her, sadness shadowing his face, and said, "I didn't realize you were so unhappy." He thought she felt like the lonely women in the story. Allison told him she wasn't unhappy, that the story was fiction.

Sometimes the problem stems from you and your need to share your work. While this is a good impulse, don't be overeager to give your writing to your significant other to read. You may be asking for trouble.

"When you begin to write," says Kate Braverman, "your husband or your daughter or your neighbor has no more idea about what you're doing than if you were studying German or Coptic. They're not in a position to evaluate your progress."

One student says, "My husband reacts very negatively to my writing at times, takes it personally, has snooped in my files and gotten mad about things I've written. I keep things secure now and he reads nothing because I never know how he will take it. That is our solution, but it leaves him out of a big part of my life. It also led to a great deal of censoring for years and kept me from cutting loose in ways I otherwise might, and that includes journals. Pretty sad overall. We did talk about it in therapy one time, not even deeply. I don't know how he deals with it now and don't ask."

Taylor Smith says, "Richard and I just decided that the marriage will last longer if he stays out of what's a no-win situation. If he criticizes, I'm apt to respond with 'What do you know?' and if he says it's great, I burst into tears and reply, 'You're just saying that because you love me.' So he reads it for the first time when the galley comes out, and if anyone asks his opinion, he says it's the best book he's ever read — since my last one. What a diplomat."

Jo-Ann Mapson, who is married to painter Stewart Allison, says, "At first when I got published, Stewart was wary of what I might reveal in my writing that could be identified with him. He doesn't feel that way anymore (he says). I know some might not agree, but my life is mine. I get to write about whatever I want because I lived through it. It's not to say I run off to tell terrible secrets, or defame anyone, but to find that emotional heart in my life and use it as a tool to make real all the stuff I think up. Art and writing make for a very good marriage for us. Without him, who knows if I ever would have written."

Stewart says, "Initially I had some problems when I would read something that I thought was 'me,' or was similar to something in our life together. It is very easy to assume that the author is just a reporter, transcribing everything directly to the page. If the husband in the story is a jerk, then *obviously* that means she thinks I'm a jerk. Eventually I came to understand that she was cooking a stew made out of me, an article in the newspaper, an incident she remembered from childhood, and lots of her own imagination. Now I have come to enjoy seeing bits and pieces of things I know mixed in among all sorts of surprises. Authors may indeed 'write what they know,' but it's not all about you. Writers' spouses need to be *very* understanding. Your author is peeling the skin off of her soul every time she sits down to write. It is humbling, frustrating, and scary work, and she deserves your support. Relax and enjoy."

Over time Brian has become a good critic, and for the most part he doesn't take the work personally. But if I think something I'm working on might be difficult for him, I don't show him until I've got a final draft, or until *after* it's published.

Yes, you've got a right to your time, space, and privacy. Your partner and kids need to understand that when you are working, you aren't available for everything they need—short of an emergency. Your honey just isn't allowed to pick up your notebook or journal or look into your computer files because he feels insecure. Likewise, you've got to respect your partner's privacy, too, and not expose aspects of his life that he wants to keep private. And if there is something he's lived through, some secret you long to use in your writing, have it be fiction and embellish the heck out of it so that no one who knows him will ever recognize what is his. And remember that it is as rude and inappropriate for a partner to engage you with small talk, demands, etc., while you're working as it is for you to space out on them when you're not.

Let your significant other know you understand how difficult it must be living with someone like you. Then demand he never look at your writing again — unless you offer it up.

set your timer

If you suspect your partner is making you feel inhibited, do this experiment. It will show you whether it's him — or you — that's inhibiting you.

Write a piece knowing full well you will absolutely show it to him afterward. Let loose and write what's on your mind and in your heart. Don't censor.

Put it aside and write version two. This one he will never see. You can even delete it before you print it out. But before you press DELETE, compare the two.

If version two is freer, more honest, and more uninhibited, decide what it will take for you to feel free to write. All it may take is his word he won't peek at your writing without your go-ahead. Or you may need a safe, an office with a locked door, or simply a password on your computer for documents you don't want him to see.

Whatever it takes, set your writing boundaries now so you will have boundless freedom to write.

living the life

The way to wealth through the quill seems long.
—Elizabeth Rundle Charles, CHRONICLES OF THE
SCHONBERG-COTTA FAMILY

marketplace madness

The marketplace can break the heart of a writer more than any other aspect of writing. We are so idealistic when we start out: Yes, we hit hard spots, reach our inner abyss, and wonder if we will be able to go on, but we somehow keep writing. Then we start sending our work out and inevitably get rejections and our self-confidence goes down the drain.

Listen up: Do not keep the marketplace in your head while you are in a creative mode. Writing with the marketplace in mind is no way to write. Learn your craft, write lots, and when you are ready, the marketplace will be ready for you.

Some students nearly drive themselves nuts about whether their writing will ever sell. But almost all of the authors I talk to on my show say they don't consider the marketplace when they're writing. Francine Prose says, "If I thought about the marketplace, I'd just kill myself right off the bat and I wouldn't write another book."

Mystery author Sara Paretsky says, "I think there's always room for good storytellers. For fifteen years I've been hearing publishers say the market is saturated for women mystery writers, and thank goodness women have not paid any attention to that and have kept right on writing."

When Janet Fitch wrote *White Oleander*, she says she wrote it for an audience of literary fiction, a *small* audience. She never dreamed it would become a megahit. "I was stunned," she says, "and I'm still stunned."

And Tracy Chevalier, author of *Girl with a Pearl Earring*, says, "I try not to give the market much thought. I had no idea so many people were fascinated by Vermeer when I wrote that book; I just knew that I was. I'm not saying market be damned, but I need readers to trust me that what I'm interested in I can make interesting for them, too."

Yes, trust yourself, and trust your readers.

Dani Shapiro, author of *Family History*, says, "Slow and steady really does win the race . . . It can be hard in grad school to remember that and even harder if you're out there laboring on your own. And it's not this big mystery — publishing! There aren't great novels sitting in drawers gathering dust because a writer couldn't find an agent or publisher. Good work does find its way. And it's not about connections. It's entirely about doing a good piece of work."

Crime writer Laura Lippman, author of *Every Secret Thing*, says, "Crime novelist Larry Block said you should always write what you want. Then, if it does really well, you have the satisfaction of enjoying commercial success because of something that was heartfelt, and if commercial success doesn't come along, well, at least you did something you wanted to do. Put your head down and keep your eyes on your own paper. Lose yourself in the process of the writing. It's frustrating and can make you crazy, but it's also really joyous, and if it's not ultimately joyous, then something is wrong."

When I think of perseverance, I think of my good friend and former student Allison Johnson. When she started as a student ten years ago, she was unpublished and quite introverted. Her writing was good, but she kept her creativity and brilliance to herself. Yet, she was one determined woman, and it paid off. She's published essays in major publications, a parenting book (*Your Self-Confident Baby*) and a novel (*The Way Home*). Allison is a study in perseverance, the first of my students who demonstrated that if you want something enough and you work your butt off, it can happen.

Facing rejection is hard, but you just never know when the tide will turn. Will you be someone who succeeds because you won't give up, or will you fail because you refuse to go the distance?

"The people who persist are the people who have a need to write that comes from inside them as opposed to someone like me who saw writing as a weapon of war," says mystery writer and journalist Andrew Vachss. "The truth about writing that nobody wants to say, but everyone knows, is, it's not a meritocracy. It's not a question of something you can measure quantitatively, like who can lift the most weight or run the fastest. There are people who have not been published who are better writers than those people who have been published."

As long as you are a writer, the marketplace will be a crow on the telephone line, cawing, creating such a cacophony it will be hard to ignore. The antidote?

In one word . . . *write.*

set your timer

What is it that you want to write? An article, essay, nonfiction book, short story, or novel?

Before you begin, do a bit of market research. If you're interested in articles, scan the article titles in your stack of magazines at home or on the newsstand. What do you see written about repeatedly? Research should show you the sorts of pieces magazine editors consider "evergreen": those topics that have the best chance of selling if you can provide a new spin. Pick one of these topics and for fifteen minutes write about how you would cover it.

Or look at the bestsellers' list. What's selling? Crime novels, romance, inspirational? Pick a topic that is hot now and write for fifteen minutes.

Does that one or any of the other topics you've noted interest you sufficiently to keep you writing? Where do *your* interests lie? Follow your own curiosities, whether they are blatantly commercial or infinitely obscure, and that's the path for you.

If you want to write a nonfiction book, research how to write a book proposal and for fifteen minutes draft the overview of your book.

Study the marketplace to see what's selling, but don't let your findings deter you from your own interests and goals. For most writers, writing *for* the marketplace is a big mistake. Trends change and just when you think you know what the marketplace wants, it's veering off in a different direction.

Writing is one thing, marketing is another.

*The act of writing is a kind of guerrilla
warfare; there is no vacation, no leave, no relief.*
—Walter Mosley, in WRITERS ON WRITING: COLLECTED
ESSAYS FROM THE *NEW YORK TIMES*

sacrifice

Most successful writers can recall the turning point of their
lives, that moment when it looked as if they would make
it as a writer.

For me, the year was 1989. I was a temporary word processor in
the office of a plant that made Kevlar parts for missiles. It was a terrible moral dilemma, working in such a place. And every day I
wanted to write and photograph, but I was broke and needed the
money. Meanwhile, I spent two or so nights a week at a public darkroom developing and printing black-and-white photos.

One night a slim young Persian man, Iraj Shadaram, arrived to
work on his pictures. We started talking. He told me he worked as a
producer at a Southern California cable TV company. He asked
what I did. I told him I was a writer.

"What kind of writer?" he asked.

Quickly, I considered his job as a producer. "A scriptwriter," I said.

It was true; although the screenplay I wrote hadn't been sold or produced, I *had* written scripts.

"*Really?*" he said. "I'm looking for a writer for a documentary on the Orange County homeless. Do you have writing samples?"

A week later I had the job. It paid shekels. I still had to work during the day at the nuke plant. After work, and into the night—sometimes all night long—I stayed at the studio or went on the street with Iraj to interview homeless people. I stood by as the crew filmed. It was exhausting, yet I loved it.

I used the tape of the documentary to get more jobs, jobs that paid well. I segued into doing other sorts of writing: copywriting, public relations writing, and brochures. I also began teaching creative writing at the Irvine Fine Arts Center, then at Upchurch-Brown Booksellers in Laguna Beach. When Travis was born, I brought the workshop into my home. I continued to write fiction and poetry on the side.

Seven years later, it was time to take another chance and try to freelance full-time for publications. I was tired of business writing; any challenge it once held had disappeared. I stopped taking on new clients and let current ones drift away.

I focused on a few magazines and newspapers. Before long, I started getting assignments. I gave up the high, relatively dependable pay of public relations writing. But I was being challenged.

I've never wanted to turn back, despite the lower pay. And I've never wanted to be one of those people who, at the end of their lives, or before, regret what they didn't do, try, or experience. Regret is a part of life, no matter what. But there are certain choices you have power over, and one of them is what you do for a living. And often— at least in the beginning, sometimes forever—being well paid and being an artist are at odds.

In my classes, I encounter folks who want to be writers, but they don't want to give up anything. They can't give up working full-time because they have car payments, house payments, vacations they want to take, dinners out they want to eat. They want to continue shopping at Nordstrom and going to expensive hairstylists and to their masseuse or facialist on a weekly basis.

Some have good reasons why they can't scale back: Their spouse isn't working, they need nice clothes for the job, they need a nice car for the job, their child is in private school. These are all valid reasons, but when you're starting out, you can't have it all. You must choose.

The life of a writer is often a life of relative sacrifice. My husband and I spend little on clothes and dining out. Our son goes to public school. We get deals on travel. We have never had a nanny. And for the first time in our eleven years together, we only recently bought a new car.

Michael Sedge, author of twenty-one published books, including *Marketing Strategies for Writers*, says, "I believe that all writers, at one point or another, have to make a decision, or sacrifice. Mine came when I quit my job and set out on an adventure to become a writer. I developed a strategy to minimize my work and increase my profits. So, take the leap. Don't look back, and make it happen. The competition is tough, and you must be even tougher."

Look at your life and make some conscious choices. Whether you love or hate your job, you must figure out a way to commit to your writing. Find a way to bring creativity into your life, even if it means writing just fifteen minutes a day. A little focus on creativity spills over and infiltrates the rest of your life. We have the opportunity daily to make small choices that we often don't use.

You don't want to be one of those people who says, "Someday I'll . . ." or someone who dreams but can't act. Or, worse yet, to someday find that you detest your life and are living with regrets you could have avoided.

set your timer

Set your timer for fifteen minutes and create two characters: one who enjoys her life and one who doesn't; one who pursues dreams and goals and one who doesn't. Seat these two at a dinner party and let them speak to each other. Each defends her position. What do they say?

Have each of them say at least once, "I'm one of those people who..." and then continue the sentence for her.

Which do you identify with? Who would you like to be?

Others may join in their conversation, but have each one represent a different point of view. See what these characters teach you about choice and internal conflict.

First publication is a pure, carnal
leap into that dark which one dreams is life.
—Hortense Calisher

literary agents

I f you have written a book—or book proposal or screenplay—
there comes a point when you must send it out into the marketplace. But you don't do the marketing yourself. That's where a literary agent comes in. Who better to market your work than someone
who earns a living that way?

To writers without one, a literary agent is one of the most exotic
and powerful of creatures. After all, agents have the power to make
your book happen—or not. No, you don't absolutely need an agent
to sell a book, but most major publishers will not even consider your
manuscript unless it comes from an agent. Besides, do you want to
spend your time writing, or marketing? Agents have access. They're
in touch with a ton of editors. They know who buys what. An agent
won't waste time sending your manuscript to editors who don't buy
the type of book you've written, no matter how good it is.

But, you may wonder, what about that 15 percent off the top that your agent gets? That money would be yours if you sold the book yourself.

True. Yet, again, you just don't hear of writers who have sold their book to a publisher themselves and received a great advance. When you hear a story about someone who found a publisher for her own book, the publisher was inevitably small and the author made little money.

In my view, agents deserve every penny they make. The good ones work for months—sometimes years—without making a dime and with no assurance that they *ever* will make a dime, sending out manuscripts, acquiring a hefty collection of rejection letters, until an editor finally says yes. If they don't sell the book, they don't get paid.

You'll find agents listed in source books such as the *Literary Marketplace (LMP)*, found at any major library, *Guide to Literary Agents* (published annually by Writer's Digest Books), and *Jeff Herman's Guide to Book Publishers, Editors, and Literary Agents, 2004*. There are other ways to find an agent: Personal referrals are great, but this means you have to get out there and network, get to know authors— and agents.

If at all possible, getting to know agents before you need their services is best of all. Signing with an agent is said to be like getting married and it is in at least one way: Your agent will forever be entitled to 15 percent of the royalties of any projects sold for you, making it necessary for you to remain in touch as long as your book is in print—hopefully forever. It's best to go with someone you know to have ethics and good judgment.

I was acquainted with my agent for at least three years before I talked to her about my current work. I talked with her on my show, interviewed her for an article, and she was a panelist at a writers' conference I chaired. You may not have these sorts of opportunities to offer agents, but you can still get to know them. Go to writers' conferences, citywide book festivals, and panels in local bookstores. In fact, if you make friends with authors, when it's time, they may recommend you to their own agent.

A good place to start is to take a class with an instructor who has publishing contacts, or even with an agent (my agent, for example, teaches in the Writers' Program at UCLA Extension and at The Loft in Minneapolis). You'll find these classes and events in the book review section of your Sunday paper, on the bulletin board or newsletter at your bookstore, online, and in college catalogs.

A conference can be a wonderful place to meet not only published authors and agents, but other writers at your same level, whatever that may be. (*Poets & Writers* magazine is a great source for conference listings.) Tom Paine, author of *The Pearl of Kuwait*, said he had been writing for ten years without success, when his brother, who was in the shoe business, said, "My people go to Vegas. Where do your people go?" Soon Paine was off to Bread Loaf Writers' Conference in Middlebury, Vermont, where he got on the writing track. He said he finally didn't feel like the odd man out because at last he was with his own sort.

Be careful and ask questions as you're searching. Don't choose an agent who charges a fee up front. All you should pay your agent for are the expenses she accrues in representing you — postage and copying costs (and some don't even charge for that). But never pay an agent to read your work or edit it. Agents take their cut once they sell the work and the check comes in.

Your potential agent doesn't have to be a New York agent, either. With the advent of e-mail, agents do business with New York publishers from all over the world. That said, you do want an agent who has contacts at major New York publishers and who travels there at least twice a year to meet with publishers. So many deals happen over lunch and through relationships built through one-on-one contact. While respectable publishers exist outside of New York, an agent without New York contacts is either new and inexperienced or not very good.

It's also not a bad idea to find an agent who is a member of the AAR (Association of Author Representatives). While there are good agents who are not members, AAR has a Canon of Ethics that agents must adhere to, or get kicked out. It's one more assurance for you that an agent is aboveboard. (On the AAR Web site at *http://www.aar-online.org*, you will find a detailed list of questions to ask an agent.)

The Web makes it easy to research agents. One Web site that's been around since 1998 is Writer Beware (*http://www.sfwa.org/beware/*). This service of the Science Fiction and Fantasy Writers of America's Committee on Writing Scams offers information on literary scams and lists agents, publishers, and book doctors who are reportedly problematic.

Once you have either a book proposal (for a nonfiction book) or a finished novel (if you're writing fiction), compile a list of agents' names and send out query letters. If you are writing fiction, include the first page or two from the novel. For a nonfiction project, a simple query will do. Always include a self-addressed stamped envelope (SASE).

Even though the query letter is essentially a business letter that talks about you and your book and why an agent should be interested, some agents, such as New York literary agent John Ware, say the writer's voice should shine through, while others, including New York agent Vicky Bijur, don't expect the query to give a sense of writing style.

"The only way you get that is from the work itself," Bijur says, "especially with fiction. However, the query letter can tell you if the author can write, spell, and is a professional, serious person. I cannot tell you how many query letters I've received that start with, 'I've written a fictional novel.' In the query letter I also want to know about the writer: What else does the writer do besides write? Is she a lawyer, a retired postal worker, a columnist? I get a zillion query letters from people who go on about their book and don't tell me anything about themselves."

And when you do submit your writing to an agent, make your first words count, whether it's your sample chapters for your nonfiction book or pages from your novel. An agent won't wade patiently through your manuscript until she gets to the good part.

"Authors are usually shocked when they hear how little we read," Betsy Amster, my Los Angeles–based literary agent, says. "But I like to compare it to the way anybody operates in a bookstore. You page through the first few pages of a novel that you pick up off the shelf and make your decision on that basis. There is no question that if you have a wonderful first sentence, that's likely to keep any agent reading longer, and if you have a terrible first sentence, they may not read beyond that."

One of the most important aspects in choosing an agent is trust. Editors talk of writers who put their professional lives in their agents' hands, but then don't trust them as they should. Agents make suggestions that authors overlook, thinking the editor is the ultimate arbiter, when, in fact, it's the agent you should listen to, in terms of changes or revisions to make to the manuscript or proposal before your agent submits it to editors.

First of all, if you don't trust your agent's judgment, you have no business signing with him or her. And second, your agent knows best how to package your project so it's best received by an editor. The mistake authors make is they overlook comments for revision their agents suggest and want their agent to submit their work anyway. Often projects are rejected for manuscript or story flaws that the agent wanted to have changed in the first place. And then it's too late for that editor; in most cases, you can't revise and resubmit to the same editor.

Of course, there are agents, and then there are agents. When I submitted my proposal to my current agent and she agreed to take me on, she was so helpful in revising the proposal. We went back and forth over two months until she felt it was good enough to send out.

I valued her input; she was once an editor at Random House, which helped me to trust her. Her ideas were all good and while I sometimes balked silently at the continued work she made me do, I was grateful for her precise eye. (Which brings up another point when looking for an agent: A former editor or someone who was involved in publishing can be a godsend.)

There's so much to know about agents; this chapter only touches on it. Do learn all you can about agents and the entire publishing process (see the bibliography for suggested reading).

And don't lose hope. Ware says, "People do want to read books. The hunger remains out there and there's always room for new talent. In the face of rejection letters, writers should hang in there and do their work and then go through the pain of application to us types. But keep the faith. Don't quit, don't go away, there is room. New writers come into print every single year. They are our lifeblood."

set your timer

Here's a nonwriting assignment for you.

Visit a bookstore and browse the acknowledgments page in novels, narrative nonfiction, how-to, travel narratives, cookbooks, or whatever genre you're writing in. Note which agents the authors thank.

This is helpful to know when it's time for you to find an agent. It's common practice to query agents who've handled a similar work.

While you're browsing, look at the writers' resource section. Look through the books mentioned in this chapter—Jeff Herman's book and the Literary Agents book—and read about what agents want. Herman's book is particularly interesting because it gives you a personal view into the lives of agents, their hobbies, and what they'd be doing if they weren't agents. This might help you fashion a query letter that stands out from the rest or even find someone who is most compatible with you.

Understanding the business of writing is vital to everyone who hopes to be published. The right agent can give you the luxury of focusing on your art, but every writer should understand the realities of the marketplace as well.

Risk! Risk anything!
Care no more for the opinions of others, for those voices.
Do the hardest thing on earth for you. Act for yourself. Face the truth.
—Katherine Mansfield, THE JOURNAL OF KATHERINE MANSFIELD

set your pen on fire

Sometimes all you have to go on is your own intuition and your own feelings about your writing. You may be having trouble breaking into national magazines or your screenplay is turned down by DreamWorks and every other major studio in Hollywood. Or if you're writing a book, you may have trouble getting an agent, or you may get one, only to find your project doesn't sell, and now you feel used and abused by the marketplace. You might even be dropped by your agent.

What then? What do you do when your hopes are dashed, when the worst, in terms of writing, has happened? Do you give up? Believe your former agent and the publishers who rejected your book? Should you throw out that manuscript, or at the very least, give it a swift kick under your bed and begin another? Or forget about writing and decide to go for your MBA, something that will ensure you make some real money? What *do* you do when everything seems to be going against you?

That depends.

I can only tell you what I did.

First, allow me to backtrack for a moment. In the late eighties, while I worked as a stress and weight counselor for a physician, I wrote a novel. I showed it to an agent I knew and she said that while she liked the writing, nothing much happened in it. The characters were too into navel-gazing, but if I could just make something happen, she'd like to see it again.

I took a good long look at its 300-plus pages and decided the story too closely mirrored my own life. I couldn't bear to spend more time with it, so I shoved it in a closet and eventually lost track of it. I probably threw it out. If nothing else, I learned the discipline of writing a novel.

I stopped working for the doctor, started temping as a word processor, wrote a TV documentary, and started getting more corporate writing clients. I also joined a writers group with published novelists—mostly in the mystery genre—and since my reading included mysteries and suspense, I started a suspense novel. Around page 100, when my heroine, Fiona, got herself into a jam and the bad guy's hand was around her throat, I learned I was pregnant. For fear I would worry my baby *in utero*, I stopped working on the manuscript. It sits out in the garage with that bad guy's hand still around Fiona's throat—poor girl.

By now I was doing PR part-time, leaving me time to write. I joined a freewriting group, figuring writing exercises were what I needed, and soon another novel—*Starletta's Kitchen*—began to take form.

A couple of years later I had finished a draft and a rewrite and showed a few agents. Some praised my writing but hated my male protagonist. I didn't like him much, either; I'd based him on an old boyfriend who said I'd be perfect—if only I got a boob job. I suppose my revenge was too over-the-top. So, I stopped sending it out and while deciding what to do about the male character, I started on a manuscript that eventually became this book.

An early version garnered the interest of an editor at a major publishing company in New York. I got an agent who hoped all she had to do was finalize the deal. It didn't work out with the publisher so my agent submitted my proposal to a handful of others. When that didn't work out, I got another agent. That didn't work out, either, for a variety of reasons. So this manuscript also went on the shelf.

But it kept nagging at me. Friends who had read parts of it would ask about it and encourage me to get it out, to work on it some more and submit it. They were sure it would sell. I wasn't sure at all. After all, it had been rejected already.

The book remained on my mind. I needed to figure out a way to make it salable. At some point I did this; I realized that it needed to be different from the rest of the books on the shelf, and I needed to share what I knew best. So I turned it from a memoir into an inspirational, instructional book and geared it specifically to people — namely women — with little time. That made all the difference.

I talked to my current agent, whom I had gotten to know, and told her about my book. She wanted to see the proposal. I made the changes I'd been pondering and a couple of months later, when the proposal was as tight as I could get it, I sent it off to her. And I waited . . . and worried. What if she didn't like it? I knew other writers she represented and I respected her taste in writing. If she hated my stuff, or was even indifferent, I'd be devastated, I was sure.

Finally, I heard from her. She said she loved it and although it might be a tough sell, she wanted to represent it, and me. She helped me get the proposal into even better shape and sent it out a couple of months later. In two weeks, we had more than one publisher interested. She set an auction for a week later. Five publishers bid on it, and Harcourt won.

All this for a project that at one point lay fallow in my garage in a file box, which I occasionally tripped over on my way to do the laundry.

My own experience tells me that to succeed with your writing, you need a combination of patience, instinct, awareness, and timing.

But mostly you need a belief in yourself and your project, and the willingness to do what it takes to work as long and hard as you must to get it out there. We often don't want to work so hard. Working hard is a pain, and selling a project involves a kind of public, shameless, extroverted activity that is not natural to most writers.

For some, working hard is easy compared to sustaining a belief in yourself and your project. Here, you might need all the support you can muster. My belief came from writer friends who offered continued support, who read chapters early on and proclaimed, "This will be published someday, it's the best thing you've ever done." I saved my notes from my writers group and took them out occasionally to be reminded: *What you have is good. What you have is worthy. Don't give up.*

I also knew the area in which I wanted to publish. I read writing books, and when I was in a bookstore, I went to the writing-book area and scanned the titles. I knew there was nothing exactly like what I was doing.

I possess a healthy amount of patience, a willingness to risk within reason, and I believe in timing. Without patience, you might as well forget being a writer, because everything in publishing, whether you're publishing a story or a poem or a book, takes a long time. There is no such thing as instant gratification.

You also have to want to write more than anything else. I love teaching, I love having a radio show, I love beading. But writing is my first love, and I knew that if I didn't do all that I could to get this book out there, I would forever regret it.

So often it's that never-say-die attitude that pulls you to the other side. Ann Packer said *The Dive from Clausen's Pier* took ten years and nine drafts.

"I became discouraged over and over again," she says, "but I kept at it because I knew it was supposed to be hard and it satisfied me in some way not to feel it was finished and not to let it go. There was something good for me in having to stay with it and not feeling it was easy or time to put it out there in the world. I do remember at one point I thought, okay, I made the mountain, now I need to climb it. I knew I didn't want those feelings that came with abandoning it."

And besides, you do know about regrets, right? They stink. You've just got to believe in yourself and not let negative voices and worries get to you. You must write despite those voices.

Robert Stone, author of *Bay of Souls*, says, "If you believe in yourself—and you must believe in yourself—you are sentencing yourself to what is, for most people, a very difficult sentence, an imperfectly rewarding life. But somebody's got to do this. Somebody's got to provide stories on a serious level for this culture, especially now. And writers are always needed. It's a profession that is honorable; it is a profession that is useful. Be brave and believe in yourself."

Yes, believe in yourself, believe in your work, and set your pen on fire every day, if you can. Write as if there is no tomorrow. And stick with it for the long haul. Be an example for your friends, your parents, your children, and for so many others who, seeing someone who stuck with it, who was courageous, who took the high road and was victorious, will go on to tell stories of their own.

acknowledgments

I owe so much to so many.

I want to thank all of my students—each and every one, past and present. I value you more than you'll ever know. You inspired this book.

Deepest appreciation to my friends and colleagues who spurred me on, one way or another: Kerry Rutherford, Noreen Ayres, Allison Johnson, Dave Mosso, Mimi Burns, Liza Samala, Glenn Goldstein, Sister Agatha Faimon, Monsignor Bill McLaughlin, the Brahma Kumaris, Judith Schwartz, Tony Eprile, the American Society of Journalists and Authors, Craig Reem, C.J. Bahnsen, Kirwan Rockefeller, Cheryl Pruett, Hugh Maquire, David Jones, Jean Femling, the Orange County Fictionaires, Martha Lawrence, Jane Anne Staw, Debbie Bull, and Andree Abecassis. And to all of the authors, poets, and literary agents who are guests on my show, especially T. Jefferson Parker, Diane Leslie, Jo-Ann Mapson, Martin J. Smith, and Barbara

Seranella; to everyone at KUCI–FM, the University of California Regents and all my listeners.

I am indebted to my instructors at Goddard College who introduced me to the writing life and wouldn't let me forget I was a writer, especially Jeff Weiss, Marc Estrin, Judith Beth Cohen, John Dranow, and Kathryn Davis.

I am so blessed to have a terrific agent, Betsy Amster, and a brilliant editor, Andrea Schulz. We have been simpatico from the start. A big thanks, also, to the people at Harcourt—Jenna Johnson, Sara Branch, Susan Amster, Rachel Myers, Tricia van Dockum, the formidable sales force, and everyone else—for taking such good care of me and putting such time and energy into my work.

I am grateful to my parents for supplying me with more material than I will ever use; Sylvia Ladeau-Bring for being the bright spot of my childhood; and Teresa Molettiere and Charlotte Dubroff, for their presence in my life.

And finally, I wish to thank my husband, Brian, who not only believed in this book when I had lost all hope, he also never lost his faith in me. I thank my son, Travis, for blessing me with his presence and wit. Not long ago he held up my tattered copy of *The Hobbit* and said, "I wonder how many rejection letters *this* one got?"

There are innumerable others who deserve thanks, so many friends, authors, and teachers since the beginning who have everything to do with where I landed. To everyone, named and unnamed, you have influenced me in untold ways. My gratitude goes out to you for always.

ॐ suggested reading

The Writing Life

Bradbury, Ray. *Zen in the Art of Writing*. Santa Barbara, Calif.: Joshua Odell Editions, 1990.

Brandeis, Gayle. *Fruitflesh: Seeds of Inspiration for Women Who Write*. San Francisco: HarperSanFrancisco, 2002.

Brown, Rita Mae. *Starting from Scratch: A Different Kind of Writer's Manual*. New York: Bantam Books, 1988.

Darnton, John, intro. *Writers on Writing: Collected Essays from the New York Times*. 2 vols. New York: Times Books, 2001.

Duras, Marguerite. *Writing*. Trans. Mark Polizzotti. Cambridge, Mass.: Lumen Editions, 1998.

Erdrich, Louise. *The Blue Jay's Dance: A Birth Year*. New York: HarperCollins, 1995.

Gardner, John. *On Becoming a Novelist*. New York: Harper & Row, 1983.

Goldberg, Natalie. *Writing Down the Bones: Freeing the Writer Within*. Boston: Shambhala, 1986.

Hemingway, Ernest. *A Moveable Feast*. New York: Scribner, 1996.

King, Stephen. *On Writing: A Memoir of the Craft*. New York: Scribner, 2000.

Krementz, Jill. *The Writer's Desk*. New York: Random House, 1996.

Lamott, Anne. *Bird by Bird: Some Instructions on Writing and Life.* New York: Pantheon Books, 1994.

Lerner, Betsy. *The Forest for the Trees: An Editor's Advice to Writers.* New York: Riverhead Books, 2000.

Levitt, Peter. *Fingerpainting on the Moon.* New York: Harmony Books, 2003.

O'Connor, Flannery. *Mystery and Manners: Occasional Prose.* Ed. Sally and Robert Fitzgerald. New York: Farrar, Straus & Giroux, 1969.

Palumbo, Dennis. *Writing from the Inside Out: Transforming Your Psychological Blocks to Release the Writer Within.* New York: John Wiley & Sons, 2000.

Plimpton, George, ed. *Writers at Work: The Paris Review Interviews.* Fifth Series. New York: Penguin Books, 1981.

See, Carolyn. *Making a Literary Life: Advice for Writers and Other Dreamers.* New York: Random House, 2002.

Ueland, Brenda. *If You Want to Write.* Saint Paul, Minn.: Graywolf Press, 1987.

Wood, Monica. *The Pocket Muse: Ideas and Inspirations for Writing.* Cincinnati, Ohio: Writer's Digest Books, 2002.

Wooldridge, Susan. *Poemcrazy: Freeing Your Life with Words.* New York: Clarkson Potter, 1996.

The Craft of Writing

Baxter, Charles. *Burning Down the House: Essays on Fiction.* Saint Paul, Minn.: Graywolf Press, 1997.

Benedict, Elizabeth. *The Joy of Writing Sex.* Cincinnati, Ohio: Story Press, 1996.

Burroway, Janet. *Writing Fiction: A Guide to Narrative Craft.* 2nd ed. Boston: Little, Brown, 1987.

Egri, Lagos. *The Art of Dramatic Writing: Its Basis in the Creative Interpretation of Human Motives.* Rev. ed. New York: Simon & Schuster, 1960.

Gardner, John. *The Art of Fiction: Notes on Craft for Young Writers.* New York: A. Knopf, 1983.

Goldberg, Natalie. *Thunder and Lightning: Cracking Open the Writer's Craft.* New York: Bantam Books, 2000.

Hale, Constance. *Sin and Syntax: How to Craft Wickedly Effective Prose.* New York: Broadway Books, 1999.

Levasseur, Jennifer, and Kevin Rabalais. *Novel Voices: 17 Award-winning Novelists on How to Write, Edit, and Get Published.* Cincinnati, Ohio: Writer's Digest Books, 2003.

O'Connor, Patricia T. *Woe Is I: The Grammarphobe's Guide to Better English in Plain English.* New York: Riverhead Books, 1998.

————. *Words Fail Me: What Everyone Who Writes Should Know about Writing.* New York: Harcourt Brace, 1999.

Marketing Your Work

Collier Cool, Lisa. *How to Write Irresistible Query Letters.* Cincinnati, Ohio: Writer's Digest Books. 1987.

Harper, Timothy, ed. *The ASJA Guide to Freelance Writing: A Professional Guide to the Business, for Nonfiction Writers of All Experience Levels.* New York: St. Martin's Griffin, 2003.

Larsen, Michael. *How to Write a Book Proposal.* Cincinnati, Ohio: Writer's Digest Books, 1997.

Page, Susan. *The Shortest Distance Between You and a Published Book: Everything You Need to Know in the Order You Need to Know It.* New York: Broadway Books, 1997.

Zobel, Louise Purwin. *The Travel Writer's Handbook: How to Write and Sell Your Own Travel Experiences.* Chicago, Ill.: Surrey Books, 1992.

Miscellaneous

Kalman, Maira. *Max Makes a Million.* New York: Penguin Putnam, 1990.

Mander, Jerry. *Four Arguments for the Elimination of Television.* New York: Morrow, 1978.

Online Resources

American Society of Journalists and Authors. http://www.asja.org

Anotherealm: Science Fiction, Fantasy, and Horror. http://www.anotherealm.com

Association of Authors' Representatives. http://www.aar-online.org

Poets & Writers: From Inspiration to Publication. http://www.pw.org

PublishersLunch. http://www.publisherslunch.com

Readerville: The Social Life of the Mind. http://www.readerville.com

Wooden Horse Publishing: Magazine News and Resources. http://www.woodenhorsepub.com